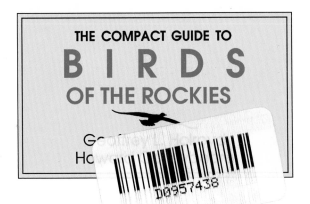

THE COMPACT GUIDE TO

B I R D S

OF THE ROCKIES

Geoffrey L. Holroyd
Howard Coneybeare

LONE
PINE

The Publisher: **Lone Pine Publishing**, #206, 10426-81 Avenue,
Edmonton, Alberta, Canada T6E 1X5

Canadian Cataloguing in Publication Data
Holroyd, Geoffrey L.
   The compact guide to birds of the Rockies
   Bibliography: p. Includes index. ISBN 0-919433-52-9

   1. Birds - Rocky Mountains, Canadian (B.C. and
Alta.) - Identification.* I. Coneybeare, Howard. II. Title.
QL685.5R6H64 1989   598.29711   C88-091599-4

Cover Illustrations: Howard Coneybeare
Cover Design: Yuet Chan
Layout: Jane Spalding
Editorial: Mary Walters Riskin
Printing: Kyodo-Shing Loong Printing Industries Pte Ltd.

Publisher's Acknowledgement
The publisher gratefully acknowledges the assistance of the
Federal Department of Communications, Alberta Culture and
Multiculturalism, the Canada Council, and the Alberta
Foundation for the Literary Arts in the production of this book.

Contents

Preface

Bird watching has been a passion for me ever since I can remember. It began in England, but I can no longer recall the origin of my interest. Was my interest stimulated by the sight of an English robin on the hospital window as I recovered from childhood surgery? Or was it the little bird books, which I still own, that told stories about the birds of Great Britain as well as serving as simple identification guides? I will never know.

What I can tell you is that my interest was intensified by little glimpses of unusual information about the lives of birds which the books provided. I read about a small dark bird that walks and swims in cold mountain streams, eating insects and minnows, and my imagination carried me away. These thirty-year-old books have few modern, North American equivalents despite the fact that our knowledge of birds has increased dramatically, to the point where the unique aspects of many species' lives are now known. What are the special interactions between species, and between birds and their environments? That is what this little book is all about.

Friends have responded to these stories with "That's neat," which is the sort of phrase I wanted this book to elicit. The book's purpose is to encourage your interest in the wildlife around you. I hope that you will enjoy our feathered neighbours more after looking through this guide, and gain an appreciation of how birds survive in the sometimes hostile Rockies.

We must leave some part of the Rockies — and indeed of the planet Earth — for wildlife, if it is to continue to exist. People protect that which they love, love that which they understand, and understand that which they are taught and experience.

I hope that you will learn from this book and experience our birds so that you will better understand, love and protect them.

- Geoffrey L. Holroyd

Acknowledgements

Geoff thanks his wife, Elisabeth Beaubien, and children Michael and Peggy, for encouragement through the hours of research and writing. He is indebted to the Canadian Wildlife Service and Canadian Park Service who provided the opportunity to spend eight years in the National Parks. The writings of Kevin Van Tighem, Brock Fenton and Michael Bradstreet inspired him to attempt the impossible and write a book.

Howard thanks John Woods, and Glenn Crowe for their valuable criticisms of the paintings. He also thanks the many others who have guided his understanding of natural history and perceptions of art, including the naturalists he worked with in Algonquin Park. He feels indebted to Canadian artists both past and present who have helped raise public awareness of the natural world and provided inspiration for the development of his own skills. These include Allan Brooks whose paintings were widely published in magazines when Howard was a child, Carl Runguis whose work he holds in highest regard, and Robert Bateman — especially for his strong public statements on critical environmental issues.

We are both indebted to Eric Bailey, who first approached us about this project, and the publisher Grant Kennedy, who believed in the book and gave it life. Mary Walters Riskin, Jane Spalding, Robin Bovey and Yuet Chan edited and produced the book. We appreciate the corrections to the text offered by Dr. James Butler, University of Alberta.

The bird checklist was compiled from records on the birds of the parks that were written by P.L. Sharp (Waterton Lakes); A.N. Wisely (Kananaskis Country); G.L. Holroyd and K.J. Van Tighem (Banff and Jasper); D.M. Poll, M.M. Porter, G.L. Holroyd, R.M. Wershler, and L.W. Gyug (Kootenay) and C. Wade (Yoho). We are indebted to these authors and all the birdwatchers whose records were used to compile the checklist.

About This Book

We have captured the stories and images of 110 bird species that are either common in the Rockies or are unique mountain specialties. This book is meant to kindle your interest in birds, while showing a plumage of each species — usually that of the adult male — to assist in identification.

Once you have seen a bird, the "brute force" index will help you to quickly locate it in the book. Keep in mind, however, that 300 species of birds have been seen in the Rockies, and only 110 are included here. Furthermore, we were able to present only one plumage for the birds we did include. If you cannot find the bird here, then refer to one of the excellent identification guides that you can find in any bookstore.

We have included a brief introduction to bird watching in the Rockies. You can find detailed guides in the book stores that will describe the trails. If you want to locate a particular bird, read the species and habitat accounts to determine the type of area that you will need to visit, then study the trail guides to locate suitable areas.

The stories about the birds included in this book come from scientific literature; most are based on articles published since 1980.

The birds appear in order of their taxonomic relationship as decided by the American Ornithologists Union, with a few exceptions such as the Western Tanager which is placed later in the book.

Bird Watching in the Mountains

As a bird watcher in the Rockies you have a formidable challenge — to look for about 300 species of birds as you hike over 3,000 kilometres of trails. You will be burdened with binoculars, field guides and notebooks, yet elated by the sights and sounds of the feathered wonders who inhabit the forest and meadows of the grey limestone mountains. After the sight of a soaring eagle or a flush of grouse the binoculars will lighten the load and seem to draw you forward to peek over the next hill or around the next corner. The mountains are a peacefully quiet place to bird watch with no chiggers and few mosquitoes. Bears are few and far between but you are wise to make sounds in the dense brush, at trail corners, or by streams. Some hikers carry bearbells as noisemakers, but they do interfere with listening for birds.

As you prepare for a hike check the trail length and grade you plan to tackle. *The Canadian Rockies Trail Guide* (1978) by Brian Patton and Bart Robinson is an excellent hikers manual for the national parks. In winter, *Ski Trails in the Canadian Rockies* (1977) by Rick Kunelius will help keep you safe on your wood slats as you take up the challenge of winter bird watching. Summer or winter, check with the local warden's office for trail conditions, fire warnings, and bear alerts. For long trips, register as you leave and when you return, and avoid hiking alone.

The old saying still applies: leave nothing but footsteps, take nothing but pictures and memories.

Bird Watchers' Ethics

All parks are here for you to enjoy and to leave unimpaired for the next visit, tomorrow or next century. Bird watchers are sensitized to the natural environment and avoid impacts on the land and its wildlife. Here is a list of "do's" to help you enjoy the outdoors.

- Use common sense, good manners and foresight in your travels.
- Leave nests and surrounding plants alone, otherwise you may cause the adult birds to desert.
- Trampling plants may make nests visible to predators, and your scent may guide predators to nests.
- Leave family groups of waterfowl, grouse and ptarmigan together. Lost young will fall prey to predators or starve.
- Stay on trails in heavily-wooded or sensitive areas such as Vermilion Lakes, Cottonwood Slough and Sunshine Meadows.
- Pick up litter.
- Keep pets on a leash.
- Leave wildflowers for others to enjoy.
- Leave fossils for others to "discover."
- Pick up stray fishing line and hooks.

Life Zones of the Rockies

The tall mountains, different rock types, and climate of the Rockies have combined to produce many varied habitats. The mountains rise into cold upper air, and expose slopes to more (southwest-facing) or less (northeast-facing) sunshine and consequent warmth. The westerly Pacific air masses bring moisture across B.C., depositing snow and rain on the Rockies. The western or main mountain ranges receive more moisture than the eastern, or front, ranges. The south-facing slopes are exposed to more sunshine, which results in dry grassy slopes that are heavily grazed by numerous large mammals such as elk, bighorn sheep, white-tailed deer and mule deer. In winter, warm air masses are regularly sucked into the prairies, resulting in the warm chinook winds that melt the valley bottom snow in the eastern part of the ranges.

The vegetation in the valley bottoms most affected by the chinook are called the montane zone. Higher in elevation, coniferous forests dominate the valley bottoms and slopes, and this is known as the subalpine zone. Above the trees is the alpine zone, the treeless splendour that has made the Rockies world famous, the region that supports many of the Rockies' specialty birds.

HABITATS

Within the Rockies there are several distinct vegetation groupings, in which different species of birds are found. Some birds have specific habitats to which they are restricted; other species occupy a variety of habitats. Below are some habitats that are easy to identify and a few birds that can be found in each.

Wetlands

Wetlands, dominated by willow, are not common in the Rockies but they do provide some of the most rewarding bird watching. These wetlands are primarily in the valley bottoms where drainage is poor and stream erosion and deposition are major factors determining the habitat's character. Open water, sedge meadows and willow shrubs provide excellent opportunities to watch birds. Look here for ducks, Osprey, kestrel, Belted Kingfisher, Eastern Kingbird, flycatchers, swallows, Common Yellowthroat, Yellow Warbler, Red-winged Blackbird, Lincoln's Sparrow and Evening Grosbeak.

Shrublands

A wide variety of shrublands can be found in the Rockies. The birds that can be found in each depends on the species of plants and the elevation. Dry, steep slopes at low elevations may be covered with shrubby cinquefoil, bearberry, and grasses; at high elevations they are dominated by juniper, willow, and bearberry. Steep avalanche slopes are typically covered in willows, stunted subalpine fir, and a variety of flowers and grasses. Rarely, slopes of alder and willow can be found at low elevation, which are productive for birding but difficult to get into. On the dense avalanche slopes listen or look for warblers: MacGillivray's, Wilson's, Tennessee, Orange-crowned, Waterthrush and Redstart. (Also listen and look for bears; grizzlies enjoy the horsetails that grow along steep streams in spring.)

In some wet valley bottoms, shrubs are dominant. White-crowned Sparrows sing from the higher branches while Harlequin Ducks hide with their young along the streams in late summer.

Grasslands

Low elevation grasslands are rare in the Rockies, but worth a visit. At higher elevations, grasslands are sparse and usually associated with seepage areas, or steep, dry south-facing slopes. This is especially true in the eastern part of the ranges below the alpine regions.

As you enter Alberta's mountain parks from the east you will drive through the larger tracts of montane grassland. Watch for Calliope Hummingbirds, Common Flickers, Vesper Sparrows, and Dark-eyed Juncos in these open areas.

Deciduous Forests

Two species of deciduous trees can be found easily in the Rockies: aspen and balsam. Typically these poplar trees grow on alluvial deposits, such as river flood plains, outwash fans, and seepage sites, all in the bottom of the lower river valleys. The ground is covered with grasses, rose bush and buffaloberry, except that some balsam forests are carpeted with horsetail or equisetum.

Aspen and balsam forests are easily found in all parks near their entrances at low elevations. Many common birds are easily found there, such as Yellow-rumped Warbler and American Robin. Other birds are not common but are most likely seen here including Ruffed Grouse and Black-capped Chickadee.

Coniferous Forests
In the montane zone, Douglas fir is the diagnostic conifer, a tree that lives on dry southwest-facing slopes that are subject to chinooks. Listen here for Western Tanagers and Solitary Vireos. Areas that have been burned in the past century tend to be dominated by lodgepole pine which succeeds to spruce forest. Many northeast-facing slopes are dominated by spruce and, at higher elevations on most slopes, by subalpine fir. Mature forests at low elevations are over 150 years old while in the upper subalpine, forests take 250 or more years to reach maturity.

In these forests you can find all of the thrush family, some warblers and sparrows and all of the owls. Gray Jays will visit you and Clark's Nutcrackers will call loudly near treeline. In the treetops you can hear crossbills and siskins.

Alpine
This zone is the most easily defined; it is that area of the Rockies above the treeline. Vegetation is sparse or nonexistent in most of the alpine, but in those few areas where soil and moisture allow, luxuriant growth is spectacular, and productive for birds, flowers, and mammals; well worth a visit. At treeline, moist slopes are covered with heather, avens, snow willow, and everlasting.

A hike to the alpine will reward you with views of

many mountain specialties. White-tailed Ptarmigan and Willow Ptarmigan (in Jasper only) can be found here. Gray-crowned Rosy Finch and Golden-crowned Sparrows can be seen feeding in the meadows. Even some species typical of the prairies occur here, such as: Brewer's Sparrow, Water Pipit and Horned Lark.

Rivers, Lakes, Streams
Open water is obviously a special habitat for many birds. Low-elevation lakes are more productive for invertebrates and fish, and consequently are popular with birds — especially waterfowl, Osprey and Bald Eagle. Higher-elevation lakes have a poorer variety of species, but Harlequin Ducks are more likely to be found there. Large rivers should be checked for Dippers which nest on small cliffs along the stream courses.

Rocks
Little vegetation and few insects can survive on the bare cliff rocks, especially at high altitudes. However, cliffs are worth checking for raven and hawk nests. You may also find Rosy Finches nesting on cliffs near alpine meadows.

Brute Force Index

The numbers correspond to the page number in the book.

Common Loon

The eerie wail of the loon is infrequently heard in the Rockies and then only near remote, low-elevation lakes that are warm enough to support sufficient numbers of fish. Unlike other waterfowl, loons continue their territorial behaviour after their eggs hatch, and chicks are raised in traditional nursery areas. On at least one occasion, an extra chick was adopted by a pair of loons. Exhausted chicks are sometimes blown across the lake from another pair. During the first two weeks, loon chicks are vulnerable to hypothermia and fatigue, so the adults carry them on their backs. This is safer than returning to the nest near shore, where predators might catch the young.

Red-necked Grebe

Grebes dive and swim rapidly using their lobed toes which are not webbed like those of ducks and loons. They dive for up to 30 seconds to depths of 7 metres (compared to 80 metres by loons), to catch insects and small fish.

Red-necked Grebes nest on lakes in the montane zone such as Vermilion Lakes in Banff and Patricia and Talbot Lakes in Jasper even though they are surrounded by human activity. Their nests, which are made of aquatic plants are often conspicuous, but should not be approached. They are normally shy birds and photographers have caused them to desert their nests. In recent years, the National Audubon Society has expressed concern about a decline in their numbers all across North America.

Western Grebe

Courtship behaviour in birds is often highly ritualized and Western Grebes are an exciting example. Each spring, pairs of grebes will run over the water side by side, in a dramatic dance with their bodies fully extended, their necks held upright and heads arched forward. Later in their elaborate courtship, pairs of grebes use the "weed ceremony," which includes neck-stretching, head-shaking, weed-diving and the breast-to-breast weed dance, ending with preening and clucking. No one knows why weeds are actually used in the ceremony.

Western Grebes migrate through the mountains in the spring when they may be seen displaying, but they are most commonly seen in the fall on the larger lakes.

Tundra Swan

The Tundra or Whistling Swan does not apparently migrate across the Rockies as some water birds do but arrives instead from the prairies. The swans are a rare migrant in the Rockies; however, flocks of up to 25 have been reported in April, May, October, and November on the larger montane lakes.

Swans have necks as long as their bodies, which enable them to reach below the water surface to feed on aquatic plants as do dabbling ducks. However, to take off, they must run across the water like diving ducks.

Tundra Swans were hunted for their feathers in the 19th century and their numbers declined. However, with protection from hunting, their numbers have increased and there are now over 150,000. The slightly larger Trumpeter Swan which is rarely seen in the Rockies is still not numerous and is considered a rare species in Canada.

Canada Goose

Geese are excellent parents. Before leaving their winter quarters the adult geese increase their weight by one-third in preparation for the rigours of the breeding season. While the male stands guard, the female incubates the eggs and she only leaves the nest to feed for half an hour each day. This may sound an excellent way to diet but she will in fact lose a quarter of her weight and become dangerously thin. After the eggs hatch, both adults travel with the goslings up to eight km to a feeding area or rearing marsh where young and adults can gain weight. With small goslings, this short trip may take four days. Once there, adults will adopt any orphaned goslings. They care for their young for about a year, with the result that around 70 per cent survive. Geese, which can live to be 30, mate for life, but may find a new mate if one dies. Watch for them in the summer on the montane lakes.

Dabbling Ducks

Pintail, Green-winged Teal, Mallard and American Wigeon are all dabbling ducks. They feed on water invertebrates and plants by tipping up their bodies and gathering food with their bills underwater. If you see puddle ducks actively feeding, their tipped up tails may initially confuse you since they don't look like birds. When these ducks take flight, they push down with their feet and with their large wings, literally jumping into the air. Both tipping up and jumping into flight are made easier by the position of their legs, near the centres of their bodies.

The males are typically brightly coloured in the spring to court the female, which is dull brown for camouflage on the nest.

Green-winged Teal

Pintail

Mallard

Pintail

American Wigeon

Green-winged Teal

Mallard

In spring, female ducks take the lead as the drakes court and follow them in apparent attempts to establish and maintain pair bonds. Even when flying, the female leads the male.

However, on landing, the male briefly takes the lead. During the egg-laying period, the female must be fertilized for each of her eggs, which are laid every other day. Males which are not her mate will try forced copulations. When landing, the male takes the lead to direct the female away from other males. If other males chase a female, she will fight, dive underwater, fly evasively, hide, or even perch in trees to escape these unscrupulous suitors.

Once Mallards have paired, the female consumes nutrient-rich snails and fly larvae. Fat reserves acquired on the wintering grounds supply her with the energy to produce the yolks, but the protein for the egg white comes from food eaten on the breeding grounds. During drought years, the need for water and protein forces Mallards to nest at higher than normal densities on the few remaining ponds, resulting in more aggression between pairs.

Mallards and Pintail are dabblers that feed in shallow water. However, on cool nights, ice can form around the edges of ponds and under such circumstances, Pintails have been recorded diving in deep water to reach food.

Pintails and Mallards are most abundant in the Rockies in April and September as they migrate from north-central Alberta to the Columbia and Fraser valleys for winter. Look for them on low elevation lakes.

Ring-necked Duck

The next eight species of ducks in this book, including this Ring-necked Duck, dive for their food of plants, fish, or aquatic organisms. The feet of diving ducks are large, webbed and placed at the backs of their bodies to allow them to swim swiftly after food to depths of 30 metres or more. However, with legs at the back of their bodies, they are awkward on land and to take off they have to run over the water surface, moving like an airplane, to gain air speed. Diving ducks have small wings and fly faster than dabbling ducks (110 km/h versus 45 km/h). Diving ducks are found in deeper lakes than dabblers, which occur along lake edges and marshes. All ducks except the Harlequin Duck are most abundant in the warmer montane lakes near the road as you enter the parks.

Lesser Scaup

Lesser Scaup arrive with most other waterfowl in early April which is when the lakes become ice-free at lower elevations in the Rockies. Curiously, scaup arrive in Manitoba in mid-April, almost two weeks after they arrive in the Rockies. Some ducks, including the scaup, come over the Rockies and spread out into the prairies, rather than flying across the Great Plains from the Gulf of Mexico. These ducks save energy by wintering closer to the Rockies and in this way avoiding the many severe spring snow storms that frequent the U.S. Midwest.

Lesser Scaup arrive early but are one of the last species of waterfowl to nest. They begin laying 9 to 12 eggs in mid-June, one egg per day. Four-year-old females lay three eggs more than one-year-old females, and fledge twice as many young. Clearly, experience at breeding is important to the success of this duck.

Common Goldeneye

Although the Rockies are within the breeding range of this duck, sightings are rare in summer. Common Goldeneye spend the winter on open stretches of the Bow, Athabasca and Waterton rivers, then fly north to breed. Over 80 have been recorded on the Banff Christmas bird count, mostly on the Bow River. In contrast, the Barrow's Goldeneye arrives here to breed in April but most have left by October. Goldeneye eat aquatic invertebrates such as larvae of caddis flies, water boatmen, dragonfly and mayfly nymphs, fairy shrimp and small fish. About a quarter of their diet is made up of plant material, which they take from the bottom of rivers.

Barrow's Goldeneye

When they arrive in April, Barrow's Goldeneye are paired but the male often continues his courting displays to maintain the female's attention. In one display, the male throws his head upward and, with his bill directed skyward, he splashes water with his webbed feet. Before copulation, the female lies prone on the water while the male performs a comical sequence of wing and leg stretches, a drink, a bill shake and a fleeting wing preen all in rapid sequence. Goldeneyes nest in trees, in the old nests left by the large pileated woodpeckers.

In the parks, Barrow's Goldeneye are found in lakes and ponds up to the treeline in spring and summer, and on large rivers in autumn.

Bufflehead

The bumblebee duck or butterball, as the Bufflehead is also known, lives in small ponds where it feeds on aquatic insects caught while swimming underwater. Although they only weigh 400 g, they can fly at 80 km/h and may live to be 13 years old. The Bufflehead nests in tree cavities of woodpeckers such as flickers. The young are coaxed out of the nest cavity by the female who leads them to the water after they fall to the ground. Young fly 50 to 55 days after they hatch. They can be seen in the Rockies between April and October at low elevations.

Harlequin Duck

The male Harlequins are avian chauvinists. They spend barely two months in the mountains before they head for the Pacific Ocean, leaving the females to care for the eggs and ducklings. Harlequins arrive on the larger rivers in pairs in early May. They display with head-nodding and short flights from rocks and gravel bars on the montane rivers. They are strong swimmers and can dive into rapids and surface upstream by using the counter-currents downstream of rocks.

The females remain until August, incubating their eggs and tending their young. Little is known about nests, so if you see one, contact the park with details.

Hooded Merganser
Common Merganser

Three species of mergansers occur in the parks. Hooded Mergansers are uncommon migrants while the Common Merganser, illustrated below, occurs more frequently and remains here to nest. The Red-breasted Merganser is a rare migrant.

Mergansers are fish eaters, and they are unpopular with some fishermen. However, their bad reputation is not warranted as half of their diet is aquatic insects and crustaceans and only half is fish. Mergansers will eat the most common fish available. While they will take sport fish if they are abundant, carp and suckers are often eaten. Size is important, as well. The smaller Hooded Merganser feeds on minnows and small fish. Common Mergansers will eat trout up to 35 cm long but they catch suckers (up to 28 cm) and even larger eels.

Both Hooded and Common Mergansers nest in holes in trees abandoned by woodpeckers. Common Mergansers will nest on cliffs such as those found in the Johnston and Red Rock Canyons, and near waterfalls, while Hooded Mergansers (illustrated above) prefer nest sites near streams. However, both species will nest wherever they find a tree hole. An important conservation project is the preservation of old trees and the provision of nest boxes near water to compensate for holes lost by forest clearing outside of our parks.

Osprey

Ospreys are easily observed in the parks in summer, catching fish and carrying them to their nests on montane lakes. The spectacular dives of the Ospreys can be appreciated all the more since they are successful about 90% of the time. The Osprey generally flies from 10 to 30 metres above the water until it sees a fish; after hovering briefly, it plunges directly at its prey, thrusting its talons down as it hits the water. Fish as large as 2 kilograms have been caught, but most of the catch is smaller. Ospreys are less successful on windy days when ripples obscure their prey.

Bald Eagle

While Golden Eagles eat red meat, Bald Eagles feed predominantly on fish. Although they will take some sport fish, most of their prey consists of fish not commonly sought by anglers.

Bald Eagles also steal from Ospreys. The eagle climbs above and dives at the Osprey, frightening it into dropping the fish. The eagle then dives after the fish, sometimes catching it before it hits the water.

You can watch Bald Eagles chasing Ospreys at the Vermilion Lakes in Banff. In April and May you may also be lucky to see Bald Eagles soaring over mountain lakes during their courtship displays.

41

Golden Eagle

Only a few of these majestic eagles nest in the Rockies. Watch for them hunting in the Columbia Icefield area and above the Kananaskis Lakes.

Males hunt alone about three-quarters of the time and successfully catch ground squirrels, hares and marmots. The rest of the time, males hunt in tandem with females, quartering into the wind low to the ground. With the male in the lead, the stronger female is in a position to catch prey flushed by the male. Curiously, the success rate when they hunt alone is one catch in three hunts, while when they hunt in tandem it is only one in about twenty. No one knows why eagles hunt in pairs when it produces such poor results.

Eagles kill many ground squirrels and hares but rarely touch larger mammals. For years they were wrongly persecuted for killing domestic sheep. In Colorado, an eagle killed a whooping crane — an unusually large prey. Today, the Golden Eagle is a protected species.

Sharp-shinned Hawk

The males of many species are larger than females, but not so with hawks. Female Sharp-shinned Hawks are almost twice as heavy as males (170 g versus 100 g). Since they are larger, females can catch larger birds than can the males, thus increasing the variety of prey that a breeding pair can catch in its nesting territory. Flight speed in birds is determined by the ratio of weight to wing area, or wing loading. Birds with high wing loading must fly faster to increase lift on the wings, which in turn enables them to stay airborne. Female Sharp-shinned Hawks have longer, wider wings to support their greater weight and as a consequence, the females fly faster than the males and can catch faster-flying prey.

Red-tailed Hawk

This hawk is not as common as it was in the 1940s, probably because of the regrowth of coniferous forests.

Although they nest high in trees, they perch lower, often on stumps or fence posts watching for mice and voles in adjacent grasslands, especially where the grass cover is not tall. As forests grow, the grassland area gets smaller and red-tails spend less time in the forested area. Red-tails hunt and protect their territory from other red-tails while soaring on warm air currents.

During cold nights, or times with little food, these hawks are able to lower their body temperature by 3°C to help conserve energy.

Northern Harrier

Although not common, the harrier or Marsh Hawk can be seen flying 3 to 10 metres above the ground as it systematically quarters over meadows for prey. Harriers prefer to hunt over open, unforested meadows and marshes. One of the more aerial raptors, this hawk flies over 100 kilometres a day searching for food. Over barren alpine meadows where visibility is unrestricted it flies at 55 km/h, but over tall grass meadows and cattail marshes where small prey are harder to spot, the hawk will slow to 20 km/h. Harriers feed on small birds, small mammals, especially meadow mice, and occasionally, injured ducks. They eat 10% to 20% of their own weight each day depending upon the temperature.

American Kestrel

You may well have seen this dainty falcon on your drive to the mountains — watch for it on power lines near highways or on dead trees in the lower valley bottoms. From its lofty perch, the kestrel watches for insects such as grasshoppers and beetles. It will also catch shrews, mice and even frogs in the fields and marshes below them.

They nest in hollow trees, usually aspen and Douglas fir, but frequent open forest and forest edges rather than the deep forest. Kestrels are dependent upon woodpeckers whose abandoned holes they claim as nest sites.

Peregrine Falcon

Historically, peregrines may have been found more commonly in the mountains; however, their decline due to DDT has resulted in the less dominant prairie falcon occurring more frequently in the Rockies.

Peregrines, which have been reported killing many raptors from the smaller kestrel to the larger Red-tailed Hawk and even Snowy Owls, are very aggressive.

Since 1976, over 170 young peregrines have been re-introduced into the wild in Alberta but few have been found nesting. If you do find a nest, report it to a park warden, ranger or conservation officer as your contribution to the restoration of this endangered species. If you are going to pass through Calgary or Edmonton from May to July, you may be able to see peregrines downtown where they now nest.

Prairie Falcon

The rare but spectacular flash of speed, power and beauty as a falcon swoops at a ground squirrel is worth the long hike to an alpine meadow. These large falcons are most likely to be seen in August and September. The prairie falcon occurs more frequently in Front Range locations such as the Cascade River valley.

If you see a large falcon, take a good look at its armpits! The Prairie Falcon's are black, while the peregrine's are light-coloured. Prairie Falcons have not been found nesting in the parks.

49

Spruce Grouse
Blue Grouse

Male grouse make poor fathers — they court females but take no part in the rearing of young. In spring, male Blue Grouse hoot to attract females to their territory. The hoot is a deep bass which does not carry far in the woods. If you hear the hoot, the grouse is nearby.

In contrast, male Spruce Grouse have an aerial display which ends with a loud crack as they slap their wings together over their back. Since this is the only sound they make, they are difficult to locate.

The female grouse returns to the male each day to have each egg fertilized. Males will mate with several females to improve the chances that their genes are passed on to the next generation.

One-year-old males will establish a territory adjacent to an older male to be nearby when he dies. Some young disperse long distances in their first year to inhabit other coniferous forests. However, once a territory is established, the grouse are very faithful to that area.

In summer, Spruce Grouse (top of opposite page) prefer closed, moist spruce forests while Blue Grouse (bottom, opposite page) prefer open spruce forests. Grouse usually remain on their summer territory year-round. (Ruffed Grouse shown below.)

Ruffed Grouse

No spring walk in the aspen forest is complete until you hear the drumming of the male Ruffed Grouse. The male stands on a log or rock and moves his wings back and forth so fast that the air vibrates.

Ruffed Grouse are primarily vegetarian — eating seeds, buds, twigs and berries of most shrubs, aspen and conifers. In summer, though, they eat insects including grasshoppers, ants and caterpillars.

In spring, and occasionally in autumn, you can hear them in aspen and mixed forests in the montane zone near the townsites. During the rest of the year, they are quiet and more difficult to find.

52

Willow Ptarmigan
White-tailed Ptarmigan

Ptarmigans are well-suited to the harsh alpine environment. Females of both species moult their feathers and colour three times a year. In winter, they are pure white with the exception of their black eyes, and bill. The Willow Ptarmigan always has black outer tail feathers. In the snow, you may see its tracks before you realize the ptarmigan is standing looking at you (see below).

In summer, the females have a brown plumage which matches the alpine vegetation around the nest. Later, grey feathers grow which act as camouflage in rocky areas.

White-tailed Ptarmigans (illustration page 54) occur throughout the Rockies in alpine areas. Willow Ptarmigans (page 55) prefer moister, shrubbier parts of the alpine and occur only in Jasper and northwards.

Ptarmigan chicks must be careful to keep warm in their cool summer homes, high in the alpine meadows. All chicks in a brood will feed at the same time. When the air temperature is between 7° and 10°C, newly hatched chicks feed for only two minutes and then must be brooded by the hen for 15 to 30 minutes to warm up. If their body temperatures drop below 34°C, they will utter distress calls, and at 32°C they become lethargic. When the air temperature is near freezing, the young chicks have difficulty feeding and keeping warm. After three weeks, the chicks have enough feathers to insulate them from the cold. If you encounter ptarmigans in the alpine meadows do not disturb the area for long, as you may increase the risk to the young.

In winter, ptarmigans roost beneath the snow. While these roosts are relatively warm and sheltered, there are hazards: wolverines may find them, and ptarmigans can break their necks as they dive into the crusty snow. Two ptarmigans were once found dead in their roost with their wings stuck together with droppings.

In winter the ptarmigans live in shrubby areas where they eat buds, catkins and fruit of willow and dwarf birch. In summer, this basic diet is supplemented with insects, grass, flowers and seeds.

In order to digest woody material, ptarmigans have long digestive tracts which extract the nutrition from the tough fibres. They are such efficient foragers that they will actually gain weight in winter when many animals have a difficult time processing food to maintain their weight.

American Coot

Coots look and act like ducks but they are actually
relatives of the rails. Like diving ducks, they feed at the
bottom of shallow lakes on vegetation rather than on
animal life. When there is ice at the edge of a pond,
dabbling ducks are unable to reach their food so some
ducks, notably American Wigeon and Gadwall, may
steal plants from coots. So as not to go hungry, some
coots abandon their first harvest at the surface and,
while the ducks squabble over it, dive again for a quiet
meal to eat some distance away.

Watch for coots out in the open water of larger lakes
swimming in large rafts of several hundred birds in
early May, September and October.

Ring-billed Gull

The two common and similar species of Ring-billed Gulls and California Gulls migrate through the mountains from their summer breeding grounds on the prairie to the Pacific Ocean. They are not easy to tell apart without good binoculars and some experience.

The abundance of gulls can be attributed in part to their opportunism. Once I watched a kestrel attack a bat in broad daylight over Lac des Arcs, east of Banff. The kestrel managed to grab the bat but was bitten in retaliation. The weakened bat was still not out of danger, as an adult Ring-billed Gull then attacked and struck the bat with its bill. The gull swooped down, picked the still bat off the water and flew off, only to be chased by other gulls trying to share the booty.

Killdeer

The Killdeer and the Spotted Sandpiper contrast markedly in their breeding strategy. Like ducklings, young shorebirds feed themselves and travel away from the nest soon after hatching. The adults avoid predators, direct the young to the best feeding areas, teach the young to feed, and keep them warm and dry until they grow a waterproof layer of feathers.

The male Killdeer establishes the territory, defends it against other males, and constructs much of the nest. The female lays the eggs and shares the incubation.

Meanwhile, the male spends time feeding and watching for predators. After the young hatch, the adults take turns watching the young and feeding away from the young. With both adults sharing the chores, the young are better protected from predators.

Spotted Sandpiper

While both adult Killdeer care for young, only one adult
Spotted Sandpiper cares for a brood — their breeding
strategy is called polyandry. The female will lay the
usual clutch of four eggs in a nest in a male's territory.
The male incubates these eggs while the female mates
with more males, laying four eggs in each territory.
Older, experienced females mate with more males than
young females. After mating with the last male, she lays
a clutch in her own territory. Thus, each adult raises a
brood separately.

   Spotted Sandpipers inhabit sparsely vegetated
habitats adjacent to streams or lakes where there is a
high density of invertebrate food. There is plenty of
food for the additional young — if they are not caught
by predators such as weasels.

Common Snipe

The Common Snipe is easy to find in spring, when the males' displays are quite obvious. The male hoots from his territory by vibrating his outer tail feathers. At irregular intervals, he will jump into the air and after a few energetic wing beats, will put his wings high above his body and glide in an arc to the ground.

More spectacular, however, is the high aerial flight. The male soars upward, winnowing as he goes. The winnowing most likely results from the vibration of the narrow outer tail feathers. Then, with wings half folded, and tail spread like a fan, the bird plummets downward back to his territory.

Great Horned Owl

Why do some owls have ear tufts? They do not help the owls' hearing since the ears are located behind the eyes, well below the tufts. One theory says that the tufts look like ears on a large mammal, and may help deter a predator. However, some species with ear tufts inhabit oceanic islands without predators. A second theory says that the ear tufts may look like broken branches and make the owls less conspicuous. Yet many species of forest-dwelling owls lack ear tufts. In short, there is no satisfactory explanation for owls' ear tufts.

Great Horned Owls are most likely to be heard in the lower valley bottoms near aspen and Douglas fir forests.

Northern Hawk Owl

The Hawk Owl is the larger of the two daytime owls.

As its name implies, it has some characteristics of the hawk: it perches on tree tops, it feeds during the day and its long tail and pointed wings are similar to a falcon's in silhouette. Unlike the nocturnal Great Horned Owl, it has no ear tufts.

Hawk Owls nest at Vermilion Pass in Kootenay National Park, in or near the 1968 burn.

Male Hawk Owls are about 5% smaller than females; nevertheless they catch the same size prey. One explanation for this reverse sexual size pattern is that female owls select males that are not aggressive, since most males attack any intruder in a territory. With sharp claws as weapons, submissive males likely make a safer partner.

Northern Pygmy Owl

The Pygmy Owl is an eruptive species in the Rockies: in some years it is relatively common but in many years it is very scarce. Like the Hawk Owl, Pygmy Owls are diurnal and frequently perch on tree tops. An opaque third eyelid protects the highly sensitive eyes from bright light, and from damage by prey, or by nestlings who may be too eager to get food.

The owl's feathered facial disks function as a pair of parabola, collecting and concentrating sound waves at the ears: thus owls can accurately detect sounds at night or from beneath the snow.

This small owl has eye spots on the feathers on the back of its head. It is thought that these spots deceive predators in the manner of eye spots on moth wings.

Boreal Owl

This secretive owl which occurs in boreal coniferous forest around the world is more common in the Rockies than was previously thought. Surveys at wardens' cabins in April and May, 1980, by the Canadian Wildlife Service found at least one Boreal Owl territory by each cabin. They call near Skoki Lodge each March and have previously been heard near Jasper townsite and along Medicine Lake. If you visit mature subalpine spruce forests in the Rockies during the spring, listen for their slow tolling, like a soft but high-pitched bell: ting, ting, ting, rising and falling. The rising and falling quality resembles a winnowing snipe. Some people consider it a dismal cry, like a wailing for the dead: hence its Latin name, *funereal*.

Great Gray Owl

The life of this large owl centres around voles in the
boreal forest. With a wing span of 1.5 metres and a body
length of one metre, this owl weighs only a kilogram.
With its large facial dishes to concentrate sound, the
Great Gray Owl listens for voles moving under the
snow then glides and catches the small rodents, which
are sometimes far beneath the surface, with startling
precision. Their courtship is complete when the female
accepts a dead vole from the male. Later, with young
owlets in the nest, the male catches voles for the female
to feed to the young. If the number of voles declines, the
owls move south to find a secure food source in winter.

Belted Kingfisher

Belted Kingfishers are found in the lower valley bottoms all year round but they are not common in winter. Unlike dippers, which can forage under the ice for small fish, kingfishers need open water to fish in winter. Then they defend a patch of open water which is abundant in fish from other kingfishers.

In summer, their territories are larger but the size is determined by the availability of cut banks where nest holes can be dug. Kingfishers prefer streams with riffles to ponds: minnows are more easily taken in riffles.

Fishermen appreciate Belted Kingfishers since kingfishers eat minnows 4 to 14 centimetres long and leave the sport fish alone.

Black Swift

Our only swift is difficult to see except at dusk as it descends to its nest. Look for them at Maligne Canyon in Jasper and Johnston Canyon in Banff. This aerial forager may travel 80 km from its nest each day at such a height that it cannot be seen. Swifts nest in the coldest parts of the canyon, near the spray of waterfalls. They lay one egg, late in the season (July) and the young take 45 days to fledge (compared to 25 for a robin). The adults feed their young flying ants which are nutritious (40% fat) but common only in August. The young are fed after dusk; they grow slowly and during the day may be torpid in the cold nest to save energy.

Rufous Hummingbird
Calliope Hummingbird

Hummingbirds seem out of place in such a cold environment, but the abundant wildflowers in the Rockies supply enough nectar to support them and their two tiny eggs, which weigh only 0.4 grams each.

Hummingbirds have a crop in which to store food for digestion on cold nights, and they can also lower their body temperatures to save energy while they sleep.

These two species contrast in body shape and territorial behaviour. The Rufous (illustrated below) is heavier (about 3.3 g compared to the 2.7 g of the Calliope which is the smallest bird in Canada). Consequently it has a higher wing-loading, resulting in faster but less energy-efficient flight. The Rufous spends

considerable time sitting on a twig-end guarding its food source. With this strategy, the rufous does not fly a great deal but can fly quickly to defend the flowers if they are invaded.

On the other hand, the Calliope Hummingbird (above) is a trap-liner — it has a larger territory which includes sparsely scattered flowers. The Calliope visits the flowers on a circuit and is constantly travelling. To make this travel less energy demanding, the Calliope has larger wings which result in lower wing-loading and slower but more efficient flight than the rufous.

Hummingbirds are hard to see — but look in nearby willow marshes where the adults perch on slender twigs, often in full view.

Hairy Woodpecker

All woodpeckers serve a dual role in forest ecology. They are voracious insect eaters, consuming ants, bark beetles and other insects, many of which are the target of insecticide spraying programs outside our parks. The woodpecker's second role is as a provider of tree cavities for other hole-nesting birds such as Tree Swallows, chickadees, Mountain Bluebirds and even Barrow's Goldeneye. None of these other species can excavate their own holes. However, even woodpeckers cannot easily excavate a hole in a strong healthy tree. Old or dead trees are vital for nest sites for all these species. In parks, such trees are left untouched but dead trees need to be left standing in forests across Canada to help preserve all cavity-nesting species.

Northern Three-toed Woodpecker

The Northern Three-toed Woodpecker most commonly occurs in coniferous forests, particularly mature spruce forest in the montane and low subalpine zones of the Rockies. Finding this woodpecker is difficult except in spring, when they drum on trees to proclaim their territory. The drumming characteristically accelerates towards the end and drops away in volume. In winter, watch for signs of their feeding: spruce trees with many bark flakes removed which litter the ground.

Other woodpeckers including the downy, hairy, pileated, flicker and sapsucker are more common in montane zone aspen forests. Aspen trees in particular tend to rot in the centre as they age and this permits woodpeckers to excavate nesting cavities with relative ease.

Northern Flicker

The Northern Flicker is one of three species in the Rockies which provide a clue to the process of how new species evolve (Dark-eyed Junco and Yellow-rumped Warbler are the other two). There are two colour forms of this species: the red-shafted form has red under the tail and wing feathers, a red moustache on the male and a brown head — the yellow-shafted form has yellow under the tail and wing feathers, a black moustache on the male and a grey head with a red crescent at the back.

The current theory is that the flickers were isolated on the east and west sides of the huge continental ice sheet until about 10, 000 years ago. Each population evolved slightly different feather colours during the ice age but the basic morphology and behaviour changed little. When the ice melted, the flicker populations reunited in the Rockies and now they freely interbreed, so consequently today you may see hybrids with colour variations of this single species.

Flickers are able to make their own nest cavity. They prefer aspen trees that are about 17 metres high with a diameter of 30 cm. Flickers make a hole 7 centimetres in diameter and a cavity 15 centimetres wide and 34 centimetres deep. These dimensions are almost identical to those used by Bufflehead, a bird that cannot make its own cavities. Unfortunately, they are also very similar to cavities used by the introduced European Starling, which in some areas uses three quarters of the available cavities.

Eastern Kingbird

The Eastern Kingbird, the largest flycatcher in the rockies, is only common in wetlands in the montane zone. They are highly territorial both toward other kingbirds and potential predators such as magpies and crows. Kingbirds will frequently lead mobbing attacks on a potential nest predator such as a crow, with a variety of blackbirds, swallows and sparrows following. Their nests are typically at the mid-height of a tree, halfway between the trunk and the leaves, to afford maximum protection from terrestrial and avian predators.

However, weather is often a critical factor that determines nesting success. Since kingbirds eat large insects which are active on warm days, they have little to catch on wet, windy and cool days which are all too common in the Rockies.

74

Olive-sided Flycatcher

Quick-three-beers, the call of this bird, is the unanswered dream of many a hot, tired and thirsty hiker as they reach treeline. Bees and flying ants are favourite foods which the flycatcher catches by darting out from a perch as the insect flies by. Olive-sided Flycatchers are one species which inhabit recently burned forests. After a fire, there are many open perches to use and the decaying wood is attractive to many insects such as ants. After a burn, insects are more available than in the unburned forest.

Least Flycatcher

Alder Flycatcher

Hammond's Flycatcher

Willow Flycatcher

Alder Flycatcher
Willow Flycatcher
Least Flycatcher
Hammond's Flycatcher

These four *Empidonax* flycatchers can only be told apart by their song, although nesting habitat does provide a clue. The Least Flycatcher's *chee-bec* call is only heard in aspen and poplar forests and shrubby wetlands. The Hammond's Flycatcher nests in coniferous woodland from the montane to the upper subalpine zones.

Hammond's Flycatcher is abundant in dry woods in Kootenay and Yoho. The less common and almost identical Dusky Flycatcher inhabits shrubby woodland such as avalanche slopes.

Young birds such as sparrows must hear their parents' songs in order to "learn" their species song, but not so the flycatchers. If a young sparrow only hears the song of another species of sparrow, it will learn a poor imitation of that song. However, Alder Flycatchers which were played the song of Willow Flycatchers, sang the alder song of *fee-bee-o* and did not mimic the *fitz-bew* of the Willow Flycatcher. These two species were thought to be one until recently as, except for their song, it is almost impossible for humans to tell them apart.

Willow Flycatchers are restricted to montane wetlands of willow, dwarf birch or shrubby cinquefoil. Alder Flycatchers can be found in montane and lower subalpine meadows vegetated with the same shrubs. Listen for them in swamps along low elevation roads.

Flycatchers catch large flying insects which only occur in summer, consequently they arrive in late May and leave in July; a brief summer in the Rockies.

Horned Lark

The Horned Lark is a small, hardy bird that arrives in the alpine of the Rockies in April. The female chooses a nest site on the leeward side of a rock or tussock. Each morning she works on the nest, digging a depression and paving the dirt with pebbles to camouflage the soil. The nest is lined with grass and soft feathers or fur.

While most small birds have naked young, the horned larks hatch with a warm covering of long, buff-coloured down. At nine days, the young leave the nest, still unable to fly, to avoid the risk of a predator finding the nest and eating the young.

Rough-winged Swallow
Bank Swallow
Tree Swallow
Violet-green Swallow
Cliff Swallow
Barn Swallow

Even though the Rockies are generally cool in summer, the supply of flying insects is large enough to attract six species of swallows. The swallows can be grouped into three pairs based on size and nest site.

The Bank and Rough-winged Swallows are the smallest. They have the largest wings in proportion to their weight, resulting in slower flight speeds than those of the other swallows. The Tree and Violet-green Swallows are heavier and have a moderate ratio of wing

Left: Rough-winged Swallow
Right: Bank Swallow

area to weight; thus they fly faster than the Bank and Rough-winged Swallows. The Barn and Cliff Swallows which are the heaviest, have the smallest wing area to weight ratio and fly faster than the other swallows.

These trends in size and flight speed are reflected in the size of prey each catches. Bank Swallows feed on small, slow flying midges which are 6 to 8 mm long; Tree Swallows catch larger midges and flies up to 12 mm, which fly faster than small midges; and Barn Swallows take heavier flies 8 to 12 mm long, which fly the fastest and supply the most nutrition. Barn Swallows have long forked tails, which they use like ailerons on aircraft to slow their flight speed and to manoeuvre close to the ground, to pick insects off grass heads.

Swallows have small feet, as do many other birds that fly continuously while hunting, because heavy feet would hinder and slow them in flight.

Bank and Rough-winged Swallows nest in holes on river banks or road cuts. Bank Swallows nest colonially, while Rough-winged nest in pairs. Tree and Violet-green Swallows nest in cavities. The Tree Swallow nests in tree cavities while the Violet-green nests in holes on rock cliffs. Finally, the Barn and Cliff Swallows make mud nests on banks, cliffs, and bridges. The Barn Swallow makes an open mud cup but the Cliff Swallow puts a mud roof on its nest and enters through a tube. All of these nests are relatively secure from predators.

Swallows are common in the Rockies. You can see them along water bodies in the montane valleys, although a few Barn Swallows build nests in the subalpine forest and a medium-sized Cliff Swallow colony lives on a high sheer rock face over Redoubt Lake in Banff.

Top to bottom:
Tree Swallow
Violet-green Swallow
Cliff Swallow
Barn Swallow

Gray Jay

The whiskey jack or camp-robber as the Gray Jay is sometimes called, visits anyone who is outdoors for any length of time in the coniferous subalpine forest.

In late summer and fall, Gray Jays collect insects, wrap them up in saliva and stick them on branches. The food items are stored singly if they are big or in clusters if they are small. Gray Jays have unusually large saliva glands to supply the sticky substance. Food stored on dead branches is less likely to be found by other birds, who generally look for food on live branches. In late winter when they are beginning to nest and food is in short supply the jays eat the scattered stores of food.

Clark's Nutcracker

Clark's Nutcracker, a striking bird of the upper subalpine, is a master of food storage. In late summer, ripening conifer seeds (Douglas fir, limber pine, and white-barked pine are their favourites), are collected and deposited in the ground. Since they cannot guard the seed store, they only put four or five seeds at each spot — not putting all their seeds in one basket. Remarkably, they store on average 30,000 seeds in 7500 sites. Even more incredible is the retrieval of these seeds in the spring as food for nestlings or fledglings: they probe the caches with an accuracy of 86%. Rodents eat about 20% of the caches, and the Clark's Nutcrackers reclaim about 70%. The remaining 10% may well grow into trees.

Watch for Clark's Nutcracker at roadside pull-offs, especially high in the mountains.

Black-billed Magpie

This colourful resident is easy to see in townsites and along major highways. It is even more common on the prairies where it has a poor reputation among farmers. Magpies will eat young birds, eggs, grain, and fruit, and peck at sores on livestock.

However, the magpie is also very beneficial. In cities, they include House Sparrows in their diet. They can be seen on the backs of bighorn sheep near Vermilion and Jasper Lakes removing ticks which would otherwise be a source of irritation and infection. As scavengers, they clean the carcasses of large mammals, reducing the risk of potential disease for other animals. In addition, the magpie's large nest, a ball of sticks, is used for shelter by robins, and as a nest site by many other birds.

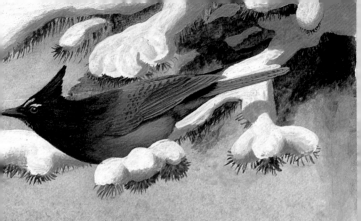

Steller's Jay

This jay is the western counterpart of the Eastern Blue Jay.

In fact, the Alberta Rockies lie between the ranges of these two species. Blue Jays are common as far west as Edmonton while Steller's Jays are more abundant in the Yoho, Kootenay, and Mount Robson Provincial Parks (immediately west of Jasper). Both species have been seen in the Alberta parks but Steller's Jay, although rare, is more frequently seen than the Blue Jay. Listen for its many raucous and hoarse calls in spruce forests of the valleys adjacent to the British Columbia border, and in the B.C. national parks.

The Steller's Jay is an omnivore, that is, it will eat most kinds of food — fruit, seeds, nuts, insects, spiders, frogs, birds' eggs, nestlings and even snakes.

American Crow

American Crows are not as abundant as the common raven in the Rockies. Until recently, crows rarely wintered in the mountains but they have been staying more frequently in the 70s and 80s because of the food available at dumps. It will be interesting to see if they become less common in Banff now that garbage is trucked away. Watch for them in the montane zone.

Flocks of crows often have a sentinel who watches for predators. Crows will chase and mob predators, especially owls. If you hear crows mobbing, quite likely there will be a harassed owl at the receiving end. It is little consolation to the owl, but crows are frequently the object of mobbing from other smaller birds such as Eastern Kingbirds and Red-winged Blackbirds.

Common Raven

You cannot spend a day in the mountains without encountering ravens somewhere, whether engaged in aerial courtship in late winter, on highway patrol for road kills in early summer mornings, or playing on the wind and performing spectacular aerobatics.

Ravens are more common now than they were 20 years ago probably because of the availability of food dumps and road kills. Up to 200 will congregate to take advantage of these food sources.

You can identify the raven by its raucous croak, wedge-shaped tail — the crow, by contrast, caws and has a round tail. The raven's black plumage absorbs the sun's rays, warming them on cold mornings.

Look for their large stick nests and the white droppings beneath on road cuts and cliffs, where they raise three or four young between April and June.

Mountain Chickadee
Black-capped Chickadee
Boreal Chickadee

Chickadees occur throughout the Rockies and are not hard to find.

The three species occupy slightly different habitats although there is also a great deal of overlap. All species occur in the coniferous forests of the subalpine zone but the Boreal Chickadee most often nests there. Black-capped Chickadees reach their highest densities year-round in aspen montane forests and willow thickets, while Mountain Chickadees are most common in Douglas fir and other coniferous montane forests.

During winter, skiers keep warm, well-fed and rested to avoid hypothermia. For chickadees, hypothermia is an important way of adapting to winter cold and restricted food supply. At night, chickadees roost in tree cavities usually singly and for up to 16 hours in the shortest days. The chickadee arrives at the hole one hour before dark, inspects the cavity, and feeds until dusk. If its mate is not roosting in the same hole it is usually less than 100 metres away, in a separate cavity. By roosting in a cavity, the chickadee is out of the cooling wind and the tree is insulation which further reduces heat loss.

The chickadee's daytime temperature is about 43°C. Within three hours of dark, the body temperature has dropped to 37°C. A six-degree drop in humans could be lethal yet the chickadee's temperature is stable at this lower level. During the night, the air in the cavity is 5°C to 8°C warmer than the outside air. In the morning, the chickadee takes about 15 minutes to warm up.

Mountain Chickadee

Black-capped Chickadee

Boreal Chickadee

Red-breasted Nuthatch

This bird searches tree bark for insects.
However, it searches a tree from the top
down, using its upturned bill to probe for
insects while in an upside-down position. The
nuthatches have two toes directed backwards to
provide grip for the downward search.

By searching a tree from the top down these
birds discover food missed by upward-climbing
birds. The nuthatch wedges nuts in a crevice to
hack them open. Hence its name nut-hack (hatch).

The Red-breasted Nuthatch is common in summer
in closed coniferous forests. In winter, it is less
common in pine, spruce and subalpine fir forests.
Listen for the nasal call, *awk-awk-awk*.

Brown Creeper

This bird is like a woodpecker, though they are not related. Like the woodpecker, it has a stiff tail which it uses as a prop, and long curved toenails. The thin bill is used to probe for insects in bark. Creepers start probing at the tree base, spiral upwards on the trunk, then glide to the base of an adjacent tree to repeat the process.

Creepers are uncommon residents of the Rockies. Their call is a high pitched *zi-i-i-it*. Creepers occur in the montane and lower subalpine zones in coniferous forests.

Dipper

The Dipper's nest is dome-shaped, built of mosses and precariously placed over a fast stream on a rock bank which is jealously guarded together with the adjacent section of stream. Since its food is locally available year-round, the Dipper can begin nesting early in the spring and often has two broods. The male will care for the first fledglings while the female incubates the second clutch of eggs.

On hot, summer days, swimming for insect larvae and small fish may seem ideal, but when it is -30°C, and humans are wearing their warmest parkas, the Dippers are still diving for food. However, the water remains above freezing and the Dipper has a well-oiled layer of feathers for protection. Look for Dippers on any mountain stream in summer and wherever there are ice-free sections of rivers in winter.

Winter Wren

Although thrushes' songs may be more pleasing to the human ear, the Winter Wren is the true master of long, complex singing.

The song of one male Winter Wren in Oregon was comprised of over 300 notes. Not only did this wren repeat his song exactly, but he sang 30 different songs, repeating each exactly as before. By comparison, male Winter Wrens in New York have only two different songs to repeat. No one knows why the western birds have so many complex songs.

To hear Winter Wrens in summer, walk in moist spruce subalpine fir forests in the Main Ranges.

Golden-crowned Kinglet
Ruby-crowned Kinglet

Kinglets are very active but surprisingly unsuspicious as they constantly move in search of insects, and insect eggs and larvae. When not nesting, they travel in mixed flocks with chickadees, creepers and woodpeckers. Both species feed up to 10 metres above the ground in coniferous forests and have similar habits, except that the Golden-crowned Kinglets exhibit a slight preference for moister, more closed spruce forests. Both species are abundant in the lower subalpine but Ruby-crowned Kinglets are more widespread in spruce trees at higher altitudes.

Kinglets can be hard to see but they are easy to hear. Golden-crowned Kinglets (see two birds on lower branches) have a thin, high *zee-zee* call, very clear and quick. The Ruby-crowned Kinglet (top two birds) is very loud with a bubbling sweet, prolonged and varied warble. Sometimes its song seems stuck on one note, repeated like a car that won't start. The Golden-crowned Kinglet is the smallest Canadian perching bird, weighing only 5 g, yet it often stays overwinter in the Rockies. Studies of kinglets in Virginia have shown that they do not have sufficient fat stores to survive a 15-hour winter night at 0°C if they maintain body temperature and do not seek shelter. Although not yet the subject of a study here, it is likely that overwintering kinglets seek well-insulated roost sites and are hypothermic at night (as are chickadees). In the Rockies, temperatures can drop to -40°C during the long winter nights and winter storms can last for several days. Survival by kinglets must be a skilled but risky business.

Mountain Bluebird

Mountain Bluebirds nest in cavities, usually in holes of montane aspen trees but also in open subalpine fir, larch forests and burnt forests (near treeline).

Bluebirds are usually monogamous, one female to one male. The male spends much of his time with the female, accompanying her on feeding trips and helping to feed the young.

Occasionally, if two cavities are present near each other, the male will accept a second female but will still spend most of his time with the first female. In one recorded instance, a second female lost her young so she helped feed the young in the first female's box. Mountain Bluebirds eat insects and berries like typical thrushes but often catch insects on the wing in the manner of flycatchers.

Townsend's Solitaire

This member of the thrush family can be seen in the Rockies all year round, although it's much more abundant in summer. During the breeding season, solitaires can be found in open coniferous forest and near avalanche slopes. Look for them in the ski areas or south-facing slopes near major highways. Like most birds, they eat a wide variety of insects, seeds, fruit and berries.

By contrast, in winter the few solitaires that remain in the Rockies have a very restricted diet of juniper berries. Solitaires are so dependent on juniper berries that they guard a patch of juniper bushes all winter, just as they guard territories around their nests in summer.

Hermit Thrush
Swainson's Thrush

One of the joys of a morning walk in June and July in spruce woods in the Rockies is the chorus of thrushes. The Swainson's Thrush (bottom) is the most eloquent with its upward spiralling song enveloping the peaks. The undulating song of the Hermit Thrush (top) is equally inspiring.

In eastern North America, Hermit Thrushes can be expected to be found only in deciduous forest and Swainson's Thrush in both deciduous and coniferous forest. In addition, both species occur at low elevations but Swainson's Thrushes also occur in the high coniferous forests while Hermit Thrushes do not. In the Rockies, this pattern does not hold true. Both species occur in coniferous forests and the Hermit Thrush is more common at higher elevations, up to treeline. At timberline, the Swainson's Thrush becomes the more common bird. It is not known why these thrushes change their preferred habitats when they reach the Rockies.

At night, thrushes roost in dense conifer trees for protection against the cold mountain air. However, they do not roost in the calmest part, which is on the lee side next to the trunk. Instead, they roost half way out on the branch, possibly to avoid predators who travel the trunk at night.

American Robin

The robin has several distinct reactions to predators, depending on the time of year and the degree of threat. During most of the year, a robin will cautiously approach a predator and watch silently for several minutes. If there is no threat, the robin will leave. Adults may also give alarm calls such as *tuk, tuk, tuk* or *teek, tuk, tuk* but keep away from the predator to avoid capture.

From April to July, adults mob predators by approaching to within one metre, making quick nervous hops, wing flicks, tail wags and loud calls. Sometimes, the robin will press home the attack, actually striking the predator. However, it is only when a predator approaches a nest that robins will mob or attack since this reaction increases the danger to themselves.

Varied Thrush

The Varied Thrush is one of the earliest songsters to
return in the spring. Its long, melancholy, quavering
whistle, pause and then second whistle higher in pitch,
can be heard from early April onwards wherever there
are mature conifer forests. Because they nest in moist
spruce forests which have well-developed shrub layers,
these thrushes are not easy to see even though they are
as common as American Robins.

The Varied Thrush, like most birds, does not heat its
unfeathered legs. Blood travelling from the toes to the
body passes by the blood heading for the toes and is
warmed. This system saves energy, especially for
thrushes with their sturdy legs.

Warbling Vireo

Warbling Vireos are heard more than they are seen as they sing their long, flowing song which sounds like *brigadier, brigadier, brigate*, repeated.

Birds in the same locality have similar songs. Young birds apparently know the basic song and need little learning to sing a recognizable song type. However, learning is very important in the development of distinct songs when they are similar to those of a neighbour.

Listen for Warbling Vireos in deciduous or mixed pine- aspen woods. They nest in the aspen tree tops usually with little leaf cover to the east and dense leaf cover to the west. In this location the nest contents are warmed early in the morning yet avoid being overheated in the afternoon.

Bohemian Waxwing

Waxwings are frugivores or fruit eaters. Except when
they are feeding insects to their nestlings, they eat fruit
of mountain ash, raspberry, rose, cedar, bearberry,
juniper and other plants. Few birds can exist solely on
fruits since they are difficult to digest and have low
nutrient content. Waxwings solve the problem, at least
partially, by digesting large quantities of berries and
fruit rapidly. Some fruits take only one minute to be
digested and expelled, others up to 30 minutes.

Bohemian Waxwings occur within the Rockies year-
round but the smaller Cedar Waxwing is not present in
the winter. Both species are more frequent in the
montane zone adjacent to wetlands.

Common Yellowthroat
MacGillivray's Warbler

You will hear more yellowthroats than you will see as they usually sit in thick bushes singing. The *wit-cha-cha, wit-cha-cha, wit-cha-cha* song of the male proclaims his territory in wetlands of willow, shrubby cinquefoil and sedges. The dull-coloured female builds the nest in the willows near water while the male distracts you with his song. During courtship, the male stops singing and the pair flies together within their territory of up to one hectare in size. The male resumes singing when the female incubates their eggs. Yellowthroats arrive in full song in early May and leave quietly in late August.

Like Townsend's Warbler, the MacGillivray's Warbler occurs only in the western forests of North America and not across the Canadian boreal forest like most warblers. MacGillivray's Warbler is most common on avalanche slopes in willow thickets. Since they are timid and stay close to the ground, listen for their liquid song which sounds like *swee-eet, swee-eet, swee-eet, peachy, peachy, peachy*. If you crouch and make a squeaking noise, the male should appear, curious about the source of the sound.

Top: Common Yellowthroat
Bottom: MacGillivray's Warbler

Yellow Warbler
Wilson's Warbler

These canary-like birds of the mountains add great colour to the willow wetlands and shrubby avalanche slopes. However, they are the unwilling hosts to the eggs of the Brown-headed Cowbird. Cowbirds lay eggs in about four of every ten Yellow Warbler nests. In three-quarters of the nests, the Yellow Warblers either bury all the eggs under a new nest or move elsewhere and re-nest. Those Yellow Warblers that nest near Red-winged Blackbirds have less trouble because the blackbirds do not tolerate the cowbirds near their territories.

If the cowbird egg is accepted, it hatches in less time than warbler eggs. The larger cowbird young takes most of the food and often pushes the smaller warbler young out of the nest. The adult warblers make about 15 trips per hour to deliver insects to the hungry cowbird which soon weighs four times as much as its foster parents.

While many species of warblers feed and nest in willow habitat, each occupies a slightly different niche. Yellow Warblers flit in the tops of willows, Wilson's Warblers can be found just below while MacGillivray's and Common Yellowthroat are usually nearer the ground.

Wilson's Warblers are widespread in the Rockies and can be found in montane willow wetlands, shrubby subalpine valley bottoms, and on avalanche slopes where they pick insects off shrubs or catch insects in flight.

Top: Yellow Warbler
Bottom: Wilson's Warbler

American Redstart

The colourful American Redstart is a common warbler in shrubby wetlands and on avalanche slopes of the Rockies. It prefers deciduous trees and is rarely seen in coniferous woods. Many species of warblers pick insects from the foliage but redstarts spend only 10% of their time looking for food in this way. Half of their foraging is done by hovering around trees to take insects from the outer leaves. They also hawk just like flycatchers — sallying forth from a perch to nab a passing insect.

Townsend's Warbler

Walking through the cool forests of the Rockies, it is hard to imagine the hot tropical jungles where many birds spend their winters. In the summer in the Rockies, Townsend's Warblers feed high in the tops of spruce trees in moist closed forest. They spend the winter in Central America catching insects in the air and on low bushes. A major conservation concern that affects the forest warblers is the cutting down of forests for lumber and agriculture both in Canada and in Central America.

Yellow-rumped Warbler

Until recently, the Yellow-rumped Warbler was considered two separate species: Audubon's, which is more common in Banff and west; and myrtle, which is more common in Jasper, and in the north and east. In the Rockies, mixed pairs are a regular occurrence, indicating that the two types are in fact only colour variations of one species.

Typically, males feed in taller trees where they sing *tsit, tsit, tsit*, followed by an energetic trill at a lower pitch. The females feed lower in the tree nearer the nest. Watch for them in all forests in the parks.

Top: American Redstart
Middle: Townsend's Warbler
Bottom: Yellow-rumped Warbler

Chipping Sparrow

Where a bird builds its nest may be critical to the survival of the eggs and young. The Chipping Sparrow, which is a common backyard bird in most Canadian communities, typically lays four eggs in its nest in a 2.5 metre high coniferous tree. The nest is usually about halfway up the tree, on the southeast side. The nestlings are warmed by the early morning sun and are protected from predominantly west winds, which conserves energy for their growth. Nestlings located on the north and west sides of trees have a higher mortality rate than those in nests on the southeast sides of trees.

Fox Sparrow

In summer, the Fox Sparrow is fairly common at treeline. Its melodious song is comprised of clear whistles followed by varied short, buzzy trills. The whistles vary from bird to bird while the end part of the trill is common to birds in each population. Thus, each song contains information about who the originator is and which population he belongs to. In this way, neighbours know each other.

A large sparrow, the Fox Sparrow feeds on the ground by vigorously kicking at leaf litter with both feet simultaneously, to expose beetles, other insects, and spiders.

Song Sparrow

Thoreau, the famous naturalist, philosopher, and writer, likened the Song Sparrow's song to this phrase: *Maids! Maids! Maids! Hang up your tea kettle-ettle-ettle-ettle*. The song does not always vary between local areas, but Song Sparrows in eastern Canada and B.C. sound very different from those in the Rockies. Our Song Sparrows look like eastern individuals rather than the large Alaskan birds, and the pale desert sparrows.

Song Sparrows have been recorded with four broods of young in one summer: a rate of one brood per month! However, the brief summer in the Rockies allows two broods at most.

Lincoln's Sparrow

In many song bird species, the nestlings learn their songs from their fathers and neighbouring males and ignore other species singing nearby. Not so Lincoln's Sparrows. They will learn some notes from neighbouring White-crowned Sparrows especially where Lincoln's Sparrows are not common. Those Lincoln's Sparrows whose songs include a few notes from White-crowned Sparrows defend their territory against individuals of both species. The mixed song may function to warn males of both species that their entry into the territory will not be tolerated. Listen for the *churr-churr-churr-wee-wee-wee-wah* of the Lincoln's Sparrow in wet sedge-willow meadows and try to identify notes from the White-crowned Sparrow's song.

Golden-crowned Sparrow

Like the Fox Sparrow , the Golden-crowned Sparrow is a summer resident of the treeline. The Golden-crowned Sparrow's song is easy to identify: listen for *oh dear me, three blind mice* sung from the tops of krummholz (stunted conifers) at treeline.

Golden-crowned Sparrows are widespread in Jasper but in Banff National Park they are not heard south of the Columbia Icefield and Helen Lake-Pipestone Pass area. They are rare in the Kananaskis and Kootenay Parks.

White-crowned Sparrow

Listen for the plaintive whistle, *more-wet-wetter-chee-zee*, of the White-crowned Sparrow. Its call can be heard in shrubby meadows all summer throughout the parks.

As you listen, try to identify minor differences between the songs of neighbouring males. If you go to other meadows, very minor variations will be evident again. Close analysis of White-crowned Sparrows over western North America has shown that the variations in their songs go back to the origins of each population during the ice ages. In these cold periods, populations of sparrows bred in isolation from each other and the songs changed only slightly over time. Now that the populations are together, these minor differences are still present and at least 18 different song types are still identifiable.

White-throated Sparrow

The attractive White-throated Sparrow with its white throat and three white head stripes is a biological

Top: Golden-crowned
Sparrow
iddle: White-crowned
Sparrow
ttom: White-
throated
Sparrow

curiosity. The species has two colour phases, one with white head stripes and one with tan stripes.

In contrast, the colour phases of White-throated Sparrows are both distributed across the Canadian boreal forest. While the white-striped males claim territory in openings in the forest and the tan-striped males are in a much broader range of habitats, they are both equally successful in raising offspring. To further confuse the issue, most males mate with a female of the opposite stripe. No one knows why there are two colour morphs. White-throated Sparrows are uncommon summer residents in the montane zone in the Rockies.

Dark-eyed Junco

Dark-eyed Junco

Dark-eyed Juncos are one of the most common birds in the Rockies. They sing loudly in most coniferous and aspen forests. After breeding, juncos flock together in groups of about twenty-five. When in small flocks, they spend a considerable amount of time scanning for predators. In flocks over 6 birds, juncos feed more and are less vigilant; however, they then spend more time in aggressive encounters with other juncos. Since most juncos are seen in flocks, it is assumed that the increased predator awareness and feeding time outweigh the disadvantages of increased aggression and competition for food.

Snow Bunting

The snow lark, snow bird or snowflake is truly a bird of winter, whether feeding over open wind-swept meadows in a prairie winter or nesting in summer snow storms in the arctic, where they occur as far north as northern Ellesmere Island.

Protected by a thick layer of feathers this 33 g sparrow will burrow into the snow, which provides added insulation from the cold night air and harsh winds of Western Canada, where -40°C is not an unusual winter temperature. Snow Buntings are a fairly common winter resident in the Rockies where they are seen along road and railway rights of way, feeding on plant seeds and wheat fallen from box cars. Up to 300 have been seen in a single flock but about 25 is a more usual number. If you miss them in the parks, watch for these flying snowflakes in fields as you drive home.

Red-winged Blackbird

The male Red-winged Blackbird arrives in the Rockies before the female, and establishes a territory with his *conc-a-ree* song. The female builds a nest, lays four eggs, incubates them and feeds young with the male's help. The pair appear to be monogamous.

However, females are sometimes seen in other male's territories. To examine this phenomenon a researcher marked pairs and vasectomized the males. The females laid eggs: and the eggs hatched. It was found that the females would breed with any nearby males while their mates did likewise with visiting females. Neither mate was monogamous.

Brewer's Blackbird

Distribution of this colonial bird is fairly restricted in the Rockies. In autumn, Brewer's Blackbirds are seen with Red-winged Blackbirds, but in summer they nest in spruce wetlands in the lower valley bottoms.

Birds often clean each other's feathers, removing lice as they do so. This behaviour is called allopreening and normally only members of the same species will do it. However, female Brewer's Blackbirds will solicit female Red-winged Blackbirds to allopreen, frequently successfully. When soliciting, the bird tucks its bill into its breast feathers and presents the fluffed nape to the redwing. Why female Brewer's Blackbirds solicit female Red-winged Blackbirds to allopreen and never the reverse, or why the males do not do it, is not known.

Brown-headed Cowbird

Brown-headed Cowbirds lay their eggs in other birds'
nests and leave the foster parents (usually warblers and
sparrows) to raise their young. In Eastern and Western
North America, cowbirds are resident and parasitize
nests within a local territory. However, in the prairies,
cowbirds feed at the feet of cattle but frequently wander
during nesting season, perhaps as a result of having
followed bison herds in the past.

Since cowbirds do not have to raise their young, the
female lays about 40 eggs over the 60 days of the
breeding season.

Rosy Finch

The Rosy Finch nests in alpine cliff crevices. Egg-laying occurs in mid-June when snow-free patches are common in the alpine meadows. The birds feed on the seeds of alpine plants. So that Rosy Finches can bring more food to nestlings, a pouch develops in their throats. Since they feed in meadows away from the nest site, they lack territories. The male Rosy Finch stays with the female, courts her and keeps other males away while she feeds. To maintain his mate, he has to stay vigilant because there are typically six males to every female Rosy Finch.

Flocks of 100 to 1000 Rosy Finches migrate through the mountain valleys in spring and autumn.

Pine Grosbeak

The short, clear musical warble of the male Pine Grosbeak, issuing from the top of a spruce tree, is one of the bonuses of spring skiing and hiking in the mountains. Besides the song of the males which is used to proclaim territories, Pine Grosbeaks have several call notes, two of which function to locate other grosbeaks. These "location" calls are only given by lone grosbeaks and end when another grosbeak arrives. Curiously, the quality of these calls varies across North America. Calls from grosbeaks recorded in Banff were ignored by grosbeaks at Churchill and vice versa. However, young from New Hampshire that were played Banff-type calls learned the new calls. Obviously, young Pine Grosbeaks learn their call-type then ignore calls from grosbeaks of other areas.

Red Crossbill
White-winged Crossbill

As its name implies, the curved bill of this bird is crossed, either to the left or the right. A crossbill feeds on cones of pine, spruce, and other conifers by wedging its bill beneath a scale: as the scale is held open, the tongue extracts the small seed. Scales on cones are arranged in clockwise and counterclockwise spirals. If the bird's upper bill overlaps to the right then the crossbill will start to eat at the base of the cone, making clockwise spirals. If the bill overlaps left, then the bird feeds in a counterclockwise spiral. The proportion of

cones with each spiral formation approximately equals the proportion of their respective overlaps, ensuring that there is adequate food for each type of bird.

The number of crossbills in the Rockies varies greatly from year to year, and depends upon the quality and quantity of spruce cones. Usually less than 10 are seen or heard in a flock but up to 30 have been recorded. They are more likely to be heard than seen. The call of the Red Crossbill (above) is a harsh *kip-kip-kip*, while that of the White-winged Crossbill (facing page) is a softer *chet-chet-chet*. Both calls are repeated a variable number of times. Listen and watch for them at Lake Louise or in the Maligne valley.

Pine Siskin
Common Redpoll

The Pine Siskin (below) is similar in many ways to the larger crossbills. Siskins feed on conifer seeds taken from cones; consequently their numbers fluctuate from year to year as do the crossbills', depending on the quantity of conifer seeds. Flocks of 10 or less are most frequently encountered but flocks of up to 100 have been seen in the Rockies. You are most likely to hear Pine Siskins as they fly over moist pine, spruce and subalpine fir forests. Listen for the *tee-ee* call repeated in flight.

Siskins migrate into the parks in April and May and leave in October. A siskin recently found dead in winter on the roadside near Revelstoke, British Columbia, had been banded two years earlier in summer in New Jersey: 3500 kilometres to the east and south!

Like other winter birds, siskins and redpolls (below) have a higher density of feathers in winter than in summer and more feathers per unit area than large birds. Both adaptations keep them warm in the cold winter. At night, siskins roost in dense conifers for protection from cold winds, while redpolls seek shelter in both dense grasses and open grasslands.

Western Tanager

If you see a male tanager, you will not forget its brilliant plumage. These birds arrive here in May from their wintering area in Central America. The female builds the nest and incubates the eggs. She spends about 21 hours a day on the nest, leaving for about 20 to 30 minutes at a time to feed. Both parents feed the young. If you are lucky enough to find a nest, the adults will simply watch you — only rarely will they scold you.

Watch for tanagers in Douglas fir forests and listen for their hoarse, robin-like call. In August when they fly south, they do not flock together and are consequently harder to see.

Evening Grosbeak

The powerful beak of the grosbeak permits this bird to open hard shells of seeds such as the sunflower or even cherry stones. Its powerful cheek muscles crack the seed by pulling the lower jaw back while the stone is held at the side of the bill. Then the stone is rolled from side to side and crushed until the seed is freed of its husk and can be swallowed. These 55 g birds can exert a 50 kilogram pressure between their bills.

Evening Grosbeaks are easiest to find and see in winter in the townsites where they feed on seeds of Manitoba maple and American ash, and sunflower seeds, at backyard feeders. If you attract Evening Grosbeaks to your backyard feeder, be prepared — they can eat hundreds of kilograms of seeds in a winter.

List of Organizations

The birds of the Rockies provide an endless source of enjoyment and study. Here is a list of organizations that can help you to further enjoy the wildlife of the Rockies:

Federation of Alberta Naturalists
Box 1472, Edmonton, Alberta T5J 2N5
(publishes Alberta Naturalist, a magazine with articles about the wildlife of Alberta)

Bow Valley Naturalists
Box 1693, Banff, Alberta T0L 0C0
(have monthly meetings in the winter, and frequent hikes in summer)

The Jasper Institute
Box 1557, Jasper, Alberta T0E 1E0
(offers field courses about the wildlife of Jasper Park)

Willow Root Nature Tours
Box 995, Banff, Alberta T0L 0C0
(this commercial company offers personal tours of the wildlife of Banff National Park)

Waterton Natural History Association
Box 145, Waterton Lakes National Park, Alberta T0K 2M0
(offers field courses about the wildlife of Waterton Lakes National Park)

In all of the parks, the park naturalists have regular hikes and evening programs that will tell you more about the wildlife of the region. Ask at the entrances to the parks and campgrounds, and check the bulletin boards in the park for more details.

Further Reading

There are many books about birds but only a few are identification guides and even fewer are good. These are my preferences.

A Field Guide to the Birds of Eastern and Central North America. Roger Tory Peterson. Houghton Mifflin Co. Boston. 1980.

A Field Guide to the Birds of Western North America. Roger Tory Peterson. Houghton Mifflin Co. Boston.

Birds of North America. Chandler S Robbins, Bertel Brunn and Herber S Linn. Golden Field Guide. New York. 1983.

Field Guide to the Birds of North America. National Geographic Society. Washington, D.C. 1983.

In addition each park has a bird checklist available from the park information centres. If you are visiting Jasper, I highly recommend *Birding - Jasper National Park*. Kevin Van Tighem. Jasper Yellowhead Historical Society. 1988.

Bird Checklist

The symbols can be interpreted as follows:

v- very rare	f - fairly common
r - rare	c - common
u- uncommon	a - abundant

Parks listed are Waterton Lakes National Park (WLNP), Kananaskis Country (KC), Banff National Park (BNP), Jasper National Park (JNP), Kootenay National Park (KNP), and Yoho National Park (YNP).

There is a column for each season: winter, spring, summer, and autumn (wssa).

Park Season	WLNP w s s a	KC w s s a	BNP w s s a	JNP w s s a	KNP w s s a	YNP w s s a
Red-throated Loon	- - - -	- - - v	v - - v	- - - -	- - - -	- - - -
Pacific Loon	- - - -	- - - -	- - - v	- v v -	- - - -	- - - -
Common Loon	v u v u	- f f f	- f f f	- f f f	- u u u	- c c c
Yellow-billed Loon	- - - -	- - v -	- - - -	- - - -	- - - -	- - - -
Pied-billed Grebe	- v u u	- - r -	- u u u	- f u f	- r r r	- - - -
Horned Grebe	- r v c	v f - f	- f r u	- u u f	- r r r	- c - c
Red-necked Grebe	- v v v	- f u f	- c u f	- c u f	- r r -	- u - u
Eared Grebe	- r v c	- u - u	- u v r	- u v r	- r - r	- r - r
Western Grebe	- r - c	- u - u	- f r f	- f r f	- r - r	- u - f
American White Pelican	- - - -	- - - -	- v - v	- - - v	- - - -	- - - -
Double-crested Cormorant	- - - -	- - - -	- - - -	- - - r	- - - -	- - - -
American Bittern	- - - -	- r r r	- r r -	- r r -	- - - -	- r r -
Great Blue Heron	- u c u	- r u r	r v u v	- v u v	- u u -	- r - u
Great Egret	- - - -	- - - -	- v - -	- - - -	- - - -	- - - -
Green-backed Heron	- - - -	- - - -	- - v -	- - - -	- - - -	- - - -
Tundra Swan	r c - c	- r - r	v r v r	- r - r	- r - -	- r - -
Trumpeter Swan	v v v v	- - r -	- - v -	- v - -	- - - -	- - - -
Greater White-fronted Goose	- - - -	- v - -	- - - -	- - - -	- - - -	- - - -

Park / Season	WLNP	KC	BNP	JNP	KNP	YNP
	w s s a	w s s a	w s s a	w s s a	w s s a	w s s a
Snow Goose	- v - r	- v - v	- r v -	- r - r	- r - r	- r - -
Brant	- - - -	- - - -	- - - -	- - - v	- - - -	- - - -
Canada Goose	r u v c	- c r c	- c c c	- c c c	- c r c	- f f f
Wood Duck	- v - -	- - - -	- r v -	- v v -	- - - -	- r - -
Green-winged Teal	- r v v	u c r c	- f u c	- f u c	- u r u	- f f f
Mallard	u c c a	u c f c	u c c c	u c c c	- c c c	r c c c
Pintail	- u v u	r f - f	v u v f	- u v f	- r r r	- f - f
Blue-winged Teal	- r r u	r f u f	v f u u	v f u u	- u r u	- f - r
Cinnamon Teal	- v v -	- r v r	- u u v	- u u -	- v - -	- r - -
Northern Shoveler	- u v r	- u - u	- u u u	- u u u	- r r r	- u - u
Gadwall	- v v v	- u - u	- u r r	- u - r	- - - -	- - - r
Eurasian Wigeon	- - - -	- - - -	- - - -	- v - -	- - - -	- - - -
American Wigeon	- c v a	- f - c	- f v f	- f - f	- u r u	- c r c
Canvasback	- - - -	- u - u	- u - u	- u - u	- - - -	- v - -
Redhead	- r v u	- u - u	- u - v	- u v -	- - - v	- v - -
Ring-necked Duck	- r r u	- f u f	- f f f	- f u u	- u u u	- f f f
Greater Scaup	- - - -	- - - -	- - - -	- r - -	- - - -	- - - -
Lesser Scaup	- u v c	- f u f	- f u f	- f u f	- r r r	- f r f
Harlequin Duck	- u u r	- u u -	- f u r	- f u r	- u u -	- f f f
Oldsquaw	- - - v	- v - -	- r - -	- u - -	- - - -	- - - -
Surf Scoter	- - - -	- r v r	- f r u	- f r u	- r - -	- f - u
White-winged Scoter	- v - r	- f r f	- f u u	- f u u	- r r r	- f - f
Common Goldeneye	u c c c	f u r u	c f - r	c f - r	- r - r	- f - -
Barrow's Goldeneye	u c c c	u u u u	r c f f	r c f f	- u r u	- c c f
Bufflehead	- u u c	r u - u	v f u u	- f u u	- c c c	- f r f
Hooded Merganser	- r v u	- r - r	- u u f	- u u f	- v - -	- r - u
Common Merganser	- c c c	u f f f	v f u f	v f u f	- u u u	- c f f
Red-breasted Merganser	- r v v	- r - r	- v - v	- v - v	- v - -	- r - r
Ruddy Duck	- v v c	- u - u	- u v r	- u v r	- v v -	- - - r
Turkey Vulture	- - - -	- - - -	- v - -	- - - -	- - - -	- - - -
Osprey	- v u -	- u u u	- f f f	- f f f	- r r r	- c c -
Bald Eagle	- u r u	- f r f	r r r u	r r r u	r u r u	u u - -

Park / Season	WLNP w s s a	KC w s s a	BNP w s s a	JNP w s s a	KNP w s s a	YNP w s s a
Northern Harrier	- c c c	- u r u	- v v f	- v v f	- r - r	- - - u
Sharp-shinned Hawk	- u u u	v u r u	v r u u	- r u u	- r r r	- u f f
Cooper's Hawk	- v u v	v r r r	v r r r	- r r r	- u u u	- u u f
Northern Goshawk	r r r r	r r r r	v r r r	v r r r	r r r r	- r r r
Broad-winged Hawk	- - v -	- r r r	- v v -	- - - -	- - - -	- - - -
Swainson's Hawk	- r r r	- r - r	- v v -	- v v -	- v - v	- - - -
Red-tailed Hawk	- c c c	- c f c	v r u r	- r u r	- r u r	- c f f
Ferruginous Hawk	- - - -	- v - v	- v v -	- - v -	- - - -	- - v -
Rough-legged Hawk	- - - -	- u - u	v v v r	v v - r	- r - u	- r - r
Golden Eagle	c c c c	r f u f	r u u f	r u u f	r u u u	- f f f
American Kestrel	- c c c	- u u u	- u f u	- u f u	- u u u	- f f f
Merlin	v v v -	- - r -	- v - v	- v v v	- r - r	r u u u
Peregrine Falcon	- - - -	- - v -	- v v v	- v v v	- - - -	- - - -
Gyrfalcon	- - - -	r r - r	- v - v	- - v v	- - - -	- - - -
Prairie Falcon	- - - -	v u u u	- - v r	- v v r	- - - v	- - - -
Gray Partridge	- - - -	v - - -	v v - v	v v - v	- - - -	- - - -
Ring-necked Pheasant	v v v v	- - - -	v - v v	- - - -	- - - -	- - - -
Spruce Grouse	c c c c	f f f f	u u u u	u u u u	c c c c	u f c c
Blue Grouse	c c c c	f f f f	v u u v	v u u v	u u u u	r u u u
Willow Ptarmigan	- - - -	- - - -	- - - -	u u u u	- - - -	- - - -
White-tailed Ptarmigan	c c c c	u u u u	f f f f	f f f f	u u u u	r f f r
Ruffed Grouse	c c c c	f f f f	v f f f	v f f f	c c c c	u f f f
Sharp-tailed Grouse	u u u u	- - - -	v - - v	v - - v	- - - -	- - - -
Yellow Rail	- - - -	- - - -	- - - -	- - v -	- - - -	- - - -
Virginia Rail	- - - -	- - - -	- v - -	- - - -	- - - -	- - - -
Sora	- - v -	- - u -	- u u u	- u u u	- u u -	- f f -
American Coot	- c v a	- a r a	v c u c	- c u c	- u u -	- f f f
Sandhill Crane	- - - -	- r - r	- - - -	- - - v	- - - -	- - - -
Whooping Crane	- - - v	- - - -	- - - -	- - - -	- - - -	- - - -
Black-bellied Plover	- - - -	- - - -	- - - v	- - - v	- - - -	- - - v
Lesser Golden-Plover	- - - -	- - - -	- v - -	- - - v	- - - -	- - - v
Semipalmated Plover	- - - -	- v - -	- - - v	- - - u	- - - -	- - - v

Park / Season	WLNP w s s a	KC w s s a	BNP w s s a	JNP w s s a	KNP w s s a	YNP w s s a
Killdeer	- c c c	v f f f	r u u f	- u u f	- c c c	- c c c
American Avocet	- v - -	- - - -	- v - v	- - - -	- - - -	- - - -
Greater Yellowlegs	- r v r	- r r r	- f u f	- f u f	- v - v	- - - -
Lesser Yellowlegs	- v - v	- r r r	- r - f	- r - f	- u - u	- r - u
Solitary Sandpiper	- v v v	- - r -	- u u u	- u u u	- u u u	- f f f
Wandering Tattler	- v v -	- - - -	- - - -	- - v -	- - - -	- - - -
Spotted Sandpiper	- c c c	- f f f	- f f f	- f f f	- c c c	- c c c
Upland Sandpiper	- v v -	- - v -	- v v -	- - v -	- - - -	- - - v
Eskimo Curlew	- - - -	- - - -	- - - -	- - v -	- - - -	- - - -
Long-billed Curlew	- - - -	- - - v	- - - -	- - - -	- - - -	- - - -
Hudsonian Godwit	- - - -	- - - -	- - - -	- - - -	- - - -	- - - v
Marbled Godwit	- - - -	- r - -	- - - -	- - v -	- - - -	- - - -
Ruddy Turnstone	- - - -	- - - -	- - - v	- - - -	- - - -	- - - -
Sanderling	- - - -	- - - v	- - - v	- - - v	- - - -	- - - -
Semipalmated Sandpiper	- - - -	- - - -	- v - v	- v - f	- - - -	- - - -
Western Sandpiper	- - - -	- - - -	- - - -	- - - r	- - - v	- - - r
Least Sandpiper	- - - -	- u - u	- - v f	- v v f	- - - v	- - - u
Baird's Sandpiper	- - - -	- f - f	- - - v	- v - f	- v - -	- - - r
Pectoral Sandpiper	- - - v	- f - -	- - - r	- v - f	- - - -	- - - r
Dunlin	- - - -	- - - -	- - - -	- v - -	- - - -	- - - -
Stilt Sandpiper	- - - -	- - - -	- - - -	- - - f	- - - -	- - - r
Buff-breasted Sandpiper	- - - -	- - - -	- - - -	- - - v	- - - -	- - - -
Long-billed Dowitcher	- - - -	- - - -	- v v u	- v - u	- - - -	- - - -
Short-billed Dowitcher	- - - -	- - - -	- - - v	- - - v	- - - v	- - - r
Common Snipe	- c c c	r f f f	v f f u	- f f u	- u u u	- c c c
Wilson's Phalarope	- v v v	- - - -	- r - v	- r v v	- v - v	- r - -
Red-necked Phalarope	- - - -	- - - v	- v v v	- r v r	- r - r	- - - u
Red Phalarope	- - - -	- - - -	- v - -	- - - -	- - - -	- - - -
Parasitic Jaeger	- - - v	- - - v	- - - v	- - - v	- - - -	- - - -
Long-tailed Jaeger	- - - -	- - - v	- - - v	- - - v	- - - v	- - - v
Franklin's Gull	- - v -	- r - r	- v - v	- r v v	- - - -	- - - -
Bonaparte's Gull	- - v -	- u - u	- r v r	- r v r	- r - r	- u u u

Park	WLNP	KC	BNP	JNP	KNP	YNP
Season	w s s a	w s s a	w s s a	w s s a	w s s a	w s s a
Sabine's Gull	- - - -	- - - v	- - - v	- v v v	- - v -	- - - -
Mew Gull	- - - -	- - - -	- - - v	- v v v	- - - -	- - r -
Ring-billed Gull	- v c a	- f f f	- u u c	- u u c	- r r r	- u u u
California Gull	- c c -	- f f f	- u u c	- u u c	- r r r	- r - f
Herring Gull	- - - -	- r r r	- r - u	- r - u	- - - -	- u u u
Thayer's Gull	- - - -	- - - v	- - - -	- - - v	- - - -	- - - -
Black-legged Kittiwake	- - - -	- - - -	- - - -	- - v -	- - - -	- - - -
Caspian Tern	- - - -	- - v -	- - - -	- - - -	- - - -	- - - -
Common Tern	- - - -	- r - r	- u r u	- u r u	- - - -	- - - -
Forster's Tern	- - - v	- - - -	- v v v	- - v -	- - - -	- - - -
Black Tern	- v r -	- - - v	- v v -	- v v -	- - - -	- - r -
Band-tailed Pigeon	- - - -	- - v -	- - - -	- - v -	- - - -	- - - -
Rock Dove	- v v -	- r u r	u u u u	u u u u	- r r r	u u u u
Mourning Dove	- u u u	- r r r	- r u r	- r u r	- u u u	- u u -
Black-billed Cuckoo	- - v -	- - - -	- - - -	- - - -	- - - -	- - - -
Flammulated Owl	- - - -	- - - -	- - - -	- - - -	- - v -	- - - -
Western Screech Owl	- - - -	v - - -	- v - -	- - - -	- - v -	- - - -
Great Horned Owl	c c c c	u u u u	u u u u	u u u u	u u u u	- r - -
Snowy Owl	- - - -	- - - -	- v v -	v - - -	- - - -	- - - -
Northern Hawk-Owl	- - - -	v v v v	r v v v	r v v v	r r r r	- r r -
Northern Pigmy-Owl	v v v v	r r r r	r u r r	r u r r	u u u u	c u u c
Burrowing Owl	- - - -	- - - -	- v - -	- - v -	- - - -	- - - -
Barred Owl	- - - -	r r r r	r r r r	r r r r	r r r r	u f f f
Great Gray Owl	r r r r	r r r r	v v v v	v v v v	r r r r	v - - -
Long-eared Owl	- - - -	- - - -	- v v -	- - - -	- - - -	- v - -
Short-eared Owl	- - - -	- - - v	r v v v	r v - v	- - v v	- - - r
Boreal Owl	- - - -	u u u u	r u r r	r u r r	u u u u	f f u f
Northern Saw-whet Owl	- - - -	f f f f	- u u -	- u u -	- r - -	- - - -
Common Nighthawk	- u u u	- u u u	- u u u	- u u u	- u u u	- r - r
Common Poorwill	- - - -	- - v -	- - - -	- - - -	- - - -	- - - -
Black Swift	- - - -	- - u -	- f f f	- f f f	- u u u	- u u -
Vaux's Swift	- - - -	- v - -	- - - -	- - - -	- r r -	- - - r

Park	WLNP				KC				BNP				JNP				KNP				YNP			
Season	w	s	s	a	w	s	s	a	w	s	s	a	w	s	s	a	w	s	s	a	w	s	s	a
Ruby-throated Hummingbird	-	v	v	-	-	-	-	-	-	-	-	-	-	v	-	-	-	-	-	-	-	-	-	-
Black-chinned Hummingbird	-	-	-	-	-	-	-	-	-	-	-	-	-	-	-	-	-	-	v	-	-	-	-	-
Calliope Hummingbird	-	c	c	-	-	-	u	-	-	r	r	r	-	r	r	r	-	r	r	r	-	r	-	-
Rufous Hummingbird	-	c	c	-	-	-	u	-	-	f	f	u	-	f	f	u	-	c	c	c	-	c	c	-
Belted Kingfisher	v	c	c	c	-	u	u	u	r	u	u	u	r	u	u	u	-	u	u	u	-	f	f	f
Lewis' Woodpecker	-	r	r	r	-	v	v	-	-	v	v	-	-	v	v	-	-	-	-	-	-	-	-	-
Red-headed Woodpecker	-	-	-	-	-	-	v	-	-	-	-	-	-	-	-	-	-	-	-	-	-	-	-	-
Yellow-bellied Sapsucker	-	c	c	c	-	u	u	-	-	u	u	r	-	u	u	r	-	c	c	c	-	u	u	-
Red-naped Sapsucker	-	-	v	-	-	-	r	-	-	-	-	-	-	-	-	-	-	-	-	-	-	-	-	-
Downy Woodpecker	c	c	c	c	u	u	u	u	u	u	u	u	u	u	u	u	r	r	r	r	u	r	-	u
Hairy Woodpecker	c	c	c	c	u	u	u	u	u	u	u	u	u	u	u	u	u	u	u	u	u	u	u	u
Three-toed Woodpecker	u	u	u	u	u	u	u	u	u	f	u	u	u	f	u	u	f	f	f	f	f	f	f	f
Black-backed Woodpecker	v	v	v	v	v	-	-	v	r	v	v	v	r	v	v	v	r	r	r	r	-	r	-	r
Northern Flicker	-	c	c	c	-	f	f	f	-	c	c	f	-	c	c	f	-	c	c	c	-	-	-	-
Pileated Woodpecker	v	v	v	v	r	r	r	r	r	u	u	r	r	u	u	r	u	u	u	u	r	c	f	u
Olive-sided Flycatcher	-	-	u	-	-	f	f	-	-	r	u	r	-	r	u	r	-	c	c	c	-	c	c	-
Western Wood Pewee	-	-	u	u	-	f	f	-	-	u	u	u	-	u	u	u	-	c	c	c	-	u	u	-
Yellow-bellied Flycatcher	-	-	-	-	-	-	v	-	-	-	v	-	-	-	-	-	-	-	-	-	-	-	-	-
Alder Flycatcher	-	-	-	-	-	u	u	-	-	r	u	r	-	r	u	r	-	r	r	r	-	u	-	-
Willow Flycatcher	-	r	r	-	-	f	f	-	-	r	f	u	-	r	u	u	-	u	u	u	-	c	c	-
Least Flycatcher	-	-	r	-	-	c	c	-	-	u	f	u	-	u	f	u	-	r	r	r	-	u	-	-
Hammond's Flycatcher	-	-	r	-	-	u	u	-	-	r	u	u	-	r	u	u	-	c	c	c	-	c	c	-
Dusky Flycatcher	-	-	r	-	-	f	f	-	-	r	u	u	-	r	u	u	-	u	u	u	-	u	r	-
Western Flycatcher	-	-	v	-	-	f	f	-	-	v	r	v	-	-	r	v	-	-	r	r	-	u	u	-
Eastern Phoebe	-	-	-	-	-	-	r	-	-	r	v	v	-	r	v	v	-	-	-	-	-	-	-	r
Say's Phoebe	-	-	v	-	-	r	r	-	-	r	r	r	-	r	r	r	-	-	-	-	-	r	-	-
Western Kingbird	-	-	v	v	-	-	v	-	-	-	-	-	-	v	v	-	-	-	r	-	-	-	-	-
Eastern Kingbird	-	u	c	u	-	u	f	-	-	u	f	u	-	u	f	u	-	u	u	u	-	f	-	r
Horned Lark	r	r	v	r	-	a	u	u	-	u	c	u	v	u	c	u	-	r	-	-	-	-	r	-
Tree Swallow	-	c	a	c	-	f	f	f	-	c	c	u	-	c	c	u	-	u	u	u	-	f	f	-
Violet-green Swallow	-	c	c	c	-	-	f	f	-	f	u	u	-	f	u	u	-	c	c	c	-	c	c	-
N. Rough-winged Swallow	-	c	c	c	-	f	f	f	-	f	u	u	-	f	u	u	-	c	c	c	-	f	f	-

Park	WLNP				KC				BNP				JNP				KNP				YNP			
Season	w	s	s	a	w	s	s	a	w	s	s	a	w	s	s	a	w	s	s	a	w	s	s	a
Bank Swallow	-	r	r	r	-	c	c	c	-	f	u	f	-	f	u	f	-	u	u	u	-	r	-	u
Cliff Swallow	-	c	c	c	-	f	f	f	-	c	c	c	-	c	c	c	-	c	c	c	-	c	c	-
Barn Swallow	-	c	c	c	-	f	f	f	-	f	f	f	-	f	f	f	-	c	c	c	-	c	c	f
Gray Jay	u	u	u	u	f	f	f	f	c	c	a	c	c	c	a	c	c	c	c	c	-	c	c	c
Steller's Jay	c	c	c	c	r	r	r	r	r	r	r	r	r	r	r	r	u	u	u	u	f	f	f	f
Blue Jay	-	-	-	-	v	v	v	v	v	v	v	v	-	-	-	-	-	-	-	-	-	-	-	-
Clark's Nutcracker	c	c	c	c	f	f	f	f	f	f	c	f	f	f	c	f	c	c	c	c	c	c	c	c
Black-billed Magpie	c	c	c	c	c	c	c	c	f	f	f	f	f	f	f	f	r	u	-	u	f	f	-	f
American Crow	v	c	c	c	u	c	f	c	r	c	v	c	r	c	v	c	v	-	r	-	-	c	c	c
Common Raven	c	c	c	c	f	f	f	f	c	c	c	c	c	c	c	c	c	c	c	c	c	c	c	c
Black-capped Chickadee	c	c	c	c	f	f	f	f	f	f	f	f	f	f	f	f	c	c	c	c	c	c	c	c
Mountain Chickadee	c	c	c	c	f	f	f	f	f	c	c	c	f	c	c	c	c	c	c	c	c	c	c	c
Boreal Chickadee	u	u	u	u	f	f	f	f	c	c	a	c	c	c	a	c	c	c	c	c	c	c	c	c
Chestnut-backed Chickadee	-	-	-	-	-	r	-	r	v	-	-	-	-	-	-	-	-	-	-	-	-	-	-	-
White-breasted Nuthatch	v	v	v	v	r	r	r	r	v	v	v	v	-	-	-	-	v	v	-	v	-	-	-	-
Red-breasted Nuthatch	c	c	c	c	u	f	f	f	u	f	f	f	u	f	f	f	c	c	c	c	u	c	c	c
Pygmy Nuthatch	-	-	-	-	-	-	-	-	v	-	-	-	-	-	-	-	-	-	-	-	-	-	-	-
Brown Creeper	r	r	r	r	r	r	r	r	r	u	u	u	r	u	u	u	-	u	u	u	f	f	f	f
Rock Wren	-	-	v	-	-	r	r	-	-	-	v	-	-	-	v	v	-	-	r	-	-	-	-	-
House Wren	-	c	c	c	-	f	f	f	-	v	v	-	-	-	-	-	-	-	-	-	-	-	-	-
Winter Wren	-	c	c	c	-	u	u	u	v	f	f	u	v	f	f	u	-	c	c	c	-	c	c	c
Marsh Wren	-	-	-	v	-	v	-	-	-	v	-	v	-	-	v	-	-	-	-	-	-	-	-	-
American Dipper	c	c	c	c	f	f	f	f	u	f	f	f	u	f	f	f	c	c	c	c	c	c	c	c
Golden-crowned Kinglet	u	c	c	c	r	f	f	f	u	c	a	c	u	c	a	c	c	c	c	c	-	c	c	c
Ruby-crowned Kinglet	-	c	c	c	-	c	c	c	-	c	a	c	-	c	a	c	-	c	c	c	-	c	c	c
Eastern Bluebird	-	-	-	-	-	-	-	-	-	v	v	-	-	-	-	-	-	-	-	-	-	-	-	-
Western Bluebird	-	-	-	-	-	-	-	-	-	v	-	-	-	-	-	-	-	-	-	-	-	-	-	-
Mountain Bluebird	-	c	c	u	-	u	u	u	-	u	u	u	-	u	u	u	-	u	u	u	-	c	c	c
Townsend's Solitaire	-	u	u	u	r	f	f	f	r	f	c	u	-	f	c	u	u	c	c	c	r	f	f	f
Veery	-	-	c	-	-	-	u	-	-	-	v	-	-	-	-	-	-	-	r	-	-	-	v	-
Gray-cheeked Thrush	-	-	-	-	-	-	v	-	-	-	v	-	-	-	r	-	-	-	-	-	-	-	-	-
Swainson's Thrush	-	c	c	r	-	c	c	c	-	f	a	f	-	f	a	f	-	c	c	c	-	c	c	u

Park	WLNP	KC	BNP	JNP	KNP	YNP
Season	w s s a	w s s a	w s s a	w s s a	w s s a	w s s a
Hermit Thrush	- c c r	- f f f	- u c u	- u c u	- c c c	- c c u
American Robin	v c c c	v c c c	r a a c	r a a c	r c a c	- c c c
Varied Thrush	- c c r	- u u u	- c f u	- c f u	- c c c	- c c c
Gray Catbird	- - c v	- - r -	- - v -	- - v -	- - - -	- v v -
Northern Mockingbird	- - - -	- - - -	- v v -	- - - -	- - - -	- - - -
Brown Thrasher	- v v -	- v - -	- - - -	- - - v	- - - -	- - - -
Bendire's Thrasher	- - - -	- - - -	- - - -	- v - -	- - - -	- - - -
Water Pipit	- c u c	- a u a	- c a c	- c a c	- c c c	- c c c
Sprague's Pipit	- - - -	- - - -	- - - -	- - - v	- - - -	- - - -
Bohemian Waxwing	v u v u	a a a a	f c f a	f c f a	u u u u	u c - c
Cedar Waxwing	- - c c	- f f f	- u u u	- u u u	- u u u	- u u f
Northern Shrike	v v - v	v - - -	r u - v	r u - v	- v - -	- u - -
Loggerhead Shrike	- v - v	- v v -	- - - -	- - - -	- v - -	- - - -
European Starling	- a a a	u c c c	u f u f	u f u f	- u u u	c c c c
Solitary Vireo	- v v -	- u u -	- u u u	- u u u	- c c c	- c f -
Warbling Vireo	- r r -	- c c -	- f c u	- f c u	- c c c	- c c u
Philadelphia Vireo	- - - -	- r r -	- - - -	- v - v	- - - -	- v - -
Red-eyed Vireo	- - r v	- u u -	- r r r	- r r r	- r r r	- r - r
Tennessee Warbler	- v v v	- u u -	- u u u	- u u u	- u u u	- r - -
Orange-crowned Warbler	- v v -	- u u -	- f c u	- f c u	- c c c	- c c u
Nashville Warbler	- - - -	- v - -	- v - v	- - - -	- - - -	- - - -
Northern Parula	- - - -	- - v -	- - - -	- - - -	- - - -	- - - -
Yellow Warbler	- c c u	- f f -	- u f u	- u f u	- u u u	- f u -
Chestnut-sided Warbler	- - - -	- - v -	- - - -	- - - -	- - - -	- - - -
Magnolia Warbler	- - - -	- r - -	- r r v	- r r -	- - r -	- v - -
Cape May Warbler	- - - -	- - r -	- - v -	- - v -	- - v -	- - - -
Yellow-rumped Warbler	- c c c	- c c c	- a a c	- a a c	- a a c	- a a f
Black-throated Gray Warbler	- - - -	- - - -	- - - v	- - - -	- - - -	- - - -
Townsend's Warbler	- u u u	- f f f	- f a f	f a f -	- c c c	- a c u
Black-throated Green Warbler	- v - v	- v - -	- v - -	- - - -	- - - -	- - - -
Palm Warbler	- - - -	- r - r	- v - v	- - v -	- - - -	- - - v
Bay-breasted Warbler	- - - -	- - - -	- - v -	- - v v	- - - -	- - v -

Park	WLNP	KC	BNP	JNP	KNP	YNP
Season	w s s a	w s s a	w s s a	w s s a	w s s a	w s s a
Blackpoll Warbler	- - - -	- r r -	- u c -	- u c -	- r r -	- u r -
Black-and-white Warbler	- - - -	- v - -	- v v -	- v - -	- - - -	- - - -
American Redstart	- u u u	- u u u	- u u u	- u u u	- u u u	- f - u
Ovenbird	- - v -	- f f -	- - - -	- - v -	- - - -	- - - -
Northern Waterthrush	- u u -	- f f -	- u u r	- u u r	- - u -	- r - u
Connecticut Warbler	- - - -	- v v -	- - - -	- - - -	- - - -	- - - -
Mourning Warbler	- - - -	- - v -	- - - -	- - - -	- - - -	- - - -
MacGillivray's Warbler	- r u r	- f f f	- u u u	- u u u	- - c u	- c c -
Common Yellowthroat	- v u v	- f f f	- f a f	- f a f	- f c f	- c c f
Wilson's Warbler	- - u v	- f f f	- u c u	- u c u	- f c f	- c c f
Canada Warbler	- - - -	- v - -	- v v -	- - v -	- - - -	- - - -
Yellow-breasted Chat	- - - -	- - v -	- - - -	- - - -	- - - -	- - - -
Western Tanager	- v c -	- u u u	- u u u	- u u u	- c c c	- c c c
Rose-breasted Grosbeak	- - - -	- r r r	- v v v	- v - v	- - - -	- - - -
Black-headed Grosbeak	- v v -	- - - -	- - v -	- - - v	- v r -	- - - -
Lazuli Bunting	- - c -	- f f -	- - v -	- - v -	- - r -	- r - -
Indigo Bunting	- - v -	- - v -	- - - -	- - - -	- - - -	- - - -
Rufous-sided Towhee	- v - -	- v - -	- v v -	- - - -	- - - -	- - - -
American Tree Sparrow	- - - v	- u - u	- v - v	- - - v	- - - -	- u - u
Chipping Sparrow	- c c u	- c c c	- c a c	- c a c	- c c c	- a c -
Clay-colored Sparrow	- c c c	- f f f	- u f u	- u f u	- r r -	- r - r
Brewer's Sparrow	- r r r	- u u u	- - c u	- - c u	- - r -	- - r -
Vesper Sparrow	- u u u	- c c c	- u u u	- u u u	- u u u	- r - r
Lark Sparrow	- - - -	- - - -	- - - -	- - - -	- - - -	- v - -
Lark Bunting	- - v -	- - - -	- v - -	- - - -	- v - -	- - - -
Savannah Sparrow	- c c c	- f f f	- f a u	- f a u	- u u u	- c c c
Baird's Sparrow	- - - -	- - - -	- v - -	- - - -	- - - -	- - - -
Grasshopper Sparrow	- - - -	- - - -	- v - -	- - - -	- - - -	- - - -
LeConte's Sparrow	- r r r	- u u u	- - - -	- - u -	- v - -	- - - -
Sharp-tailed Sparrow	- - - -	- - - -	- - - v	- - - -	- - - -	- - - -
Fox Sparrow	- c c c	- f f f	- u f u	- u f u	- c c c	- f f f
Song Sparrow	- r u r	- u u u	v u f u	v u f u	- u r u	- u - u

Park	WLNP	KC	BNP	JNP	KNP	YNP
Season	ws s a	ws s a	ws s a	ws s a	ws s a	ws s a
Lincoln's Sparrow	- v u v	- f f f	- f a f	- f a f	- f c f	- c c f
Swamp Sparrow	- - - -	- v - -	- v - v	- v v -	- - - -	- - - -
White-throated Sparrow	- r - -	v u r u	v r u r	v r u r	- - - -	- - - -
Golden-crowned Sparrow	- - - -	- r - r	- u f u	- u f u	- - v -	- - - -
White-crowned Sparrow	- c c c	r c c c	v c a c	v c a c	- u u u	- c c c
Harris' Sparrow	- - - -	- r - r	- r - r	- r - r	- r - -	- - - -
Dark-eyed Junco	- c c c	r c c c	r a a c	- a a c	r c c c	r c a f
Lapland Longspur	- - - -	v r - r	- v - u	- v - u	- - - -	- - - u
Chestnut-collared Longspur	- v v -	- - - -	- v - -	- - - -	- - - -	- - - -
Snow Bunting	u r - r	f c - c	c r - r	c r - r	- u - u	f f - f
Bobolink	- v v -	- r r -	- r v -	- - - -	- - - -	- r - -
Red-winged Blackbird	- c c c	- c c c	r c c f	r c c f	- c c c	- c c -
Western Meadowlark	- c c u	- u u u	- r v -	- r v v	- u r -	- u - u
Yellow-headed Blackbird	- r r r	- r - r	- u v v	- u v -	- r r -	- u - -
Rusty Blackbird	- - - -	v u - u	v r - r	v r v r	- - - v	- u - u
Brewer's Blackbird	- c c u	v u u u	r f c f	- f c f	- r r -	- f u f
Common Grackle	- - v -	- r - r	- - - v	- v - -	- - - -	- r - -
Brown-headed Cowbird	- c c -	- c c c	- c c c	- c c c	- u u u	- u u u
Northern Oriole	- v v -	- r r r	- - v -	- r v -	- - - -	- - - -
Rosy Finch	v c c c	v f u f	v c a c	v c a c	- c c c	f f f f
Pine Grosbeak	u u u u	u u u u	f f c f	f f c f	c c c c	f f c f
Purple Finch	- v v -	- r r r	v f u r	- f u r	- u u -	- r - r
Cassin's Finch	- v v -	- u u u	- r r -	- v - v	- r r -	- r r -
House Finch	- - v -	- - v -	- - - -	- v - -	- - - -	- - - -
Red Crossbill	- - v v	u u u u	f f f f	f f f f	u u u u	f f f f
White-winged Crossbill	- - v v	f f f f	f f f f	f f f f	u u u u	f f f f
Hoary Redpoll	v v - v	r - - -	u u - -	u u - -	- - - -	- - - -
Common Redpoll	u u - -	c - - -	c c v c	c c - c	u u - u	f f - f
American Goldfinch	- r c r	- - u -	- v v v	- - - -	- v v -	- r - r
Pine Siskin	v c c c	- c c c	r c a c	r c a c	- c c c	- f a u
Evening Grosbeak	- r r r	f r r r	u u u u	u u u u	- c c c	- u u u
House Sparrow	v c c c	a a a a	f f f f	f f f f	- - v v	c c c c

Index

About the Author

Geoff Holroyd was born in Yorkshire, England and raised in Toronto. In 1961 he began 15 years as a volunteer with the Long Point Bird Observatory of Ontario, ultimately becoming chairman of the board of directors from 1970 to 1973. He completed his Ph.D. at the University of Toronto. In 1975 he moved to Banff and began work for the Canadian Wildlife Service on the Ecological Wildlife Inventories of Banff, Jasper, Kootenay, Glacier and Revelstoke National Parks. In 1983 he became head of the Threatened Species Conservation Section of the Canadian Wildlife Service in Edmonton. Geoff is currently a research scientist at Canadian Wildlife Service, an adjunct professor at the University of Alberta, and serves on the boards of several wildlife and conservation groups.

About the Illustrator

Howard Coneybeare grew up on a farm in Southern Ontario. He began studying taxidermy at the age of 13. He received his B.Sc. with Honours from the University of Guelph, where he also studied art. In 1970 he began working as a summer naturalist in Algonquin Park, and prepared his first ink illustrations for some of the park's publications. He continued his art training at the University of Alberta and the Alberta College of Art. He also worked two summers on a wildlife inventory project in Banff National Park. Currently he works as an exhibit designer for National Parks of Canada, and lives near Cochrane, Alberta. He works principally in acrylic paints and screenprinting media. His interests include birding, botany, hiking, and photography.